Hugh Latimer

Sermons on the Card and other discourses

Hugh Latimer

Sermons on the Card and other discourses

ISBN/EAN: 9783744745499

Printed in Europe, USA, Canada, Australia, Japan

Cover: Foto ©Lupo / pixelio.de

More available books at **www.hansebooks.com**

CASSELL'S NATIONAL LIBRARY.

SERMONS ON THE CARD

AND OTHER DISCOURSES.

BY

HUGH LATIMER,

SOMETIME BISHOP OF WORCESTER,
MARTYR, 1555.

CASSELL & COMPANY, Limited:
LONDON, PARIS, NEW YORK & MELBOURNE.
1883.

INTRODUCTION.

Hugh Latimer, a farmer's son, was born about the year 1491, at Thurcaston, in Leicestershire. He was an only son, with six sisters, who were all well cared for at home. He was a boy of fourteen when sent to Clare College, Cambridge. When about twenty-four years old, he had obtained a college fellowship, had taken the degree of Master of Arts, and was ordained Priest of the Roman Church at Lincoln. In 1524, at the age of about thirty, he proceeded to the degree of B.D., and on the occasion of his doing so he argued publicly for the Pope's authority against opinions of Melancthon. Thomas Bilney went afterwards to Latimer's rooms, gave him his own reasons for goodwill to the teaching of Melancthon, and explained to him his faith as a Reformer in a way that secured Latimer's attention. Latimer's free, vigorous mind admitted the new reasonings, and in his after-life he looked always upon "little Bilney" as the man who had first opened his eyes.

With homely earnestness Latimer began soon to express his new convictions. His zeal and purity of life had caused him to be trusted by the University as a maintainer of old ways; he had been appointed cross-bearer to the University, and elected one of the twelve preachers annually appointed in obedience to a bull of Pope Alexander VI. Now Latimer walked and worked with Bilney, visiting the sick and the prisoners, and reasoning together of the needs of Christendom. The Bishop of the diocese presently forbade Latimer's preaching in any of the pulpits of the University. Robert Barnes, prior of the Augustinian Friars at Cambridge, a man stirred to the depths by the new movement of thought, then invited Latimer to preach in the church of the Augustinians. Latimer was next summoned before Wolsey, whom he satisfied so well that Wolsey overruled the Bishop's inhibition, and Latimer again became a free preacher in Cambridge.

The influence of Latimer's preaching became every year greater; and in December, 1529, he gave occasion to new controversy in the University by his two Sermons on the Card, delivered in St. Edward's Church, on the Sunday before Christmas, 1529. Card-playing was in those days an amusement especially favoured at Christmas time. Latimer does not express disapproval, though the Reformers generally were opposed to it. The early statutes of St. John's College, Cambridge, forbade playing with dice or cards by members of the college at any time except Christmas, but excluded undergraduates even from the Christmas privilege. In these sermons Latimer used the card-playing of the season for illustrations of spiritual truth drawn from the trump card in triumph, and the rules of the game of primero. His homely parables enforced views of religious duty more in accordance with the mind of the Reformers than of those who held by the old ways. The Prior of the Dominicans at Cambridge tried to answer Latimer's sermon on the cards with an antagonistic sermon on the dice: the orthodox Christian was to win by a throw of cinque and quatre—the cinque, five texts to be quoted against Luther; and the quatre the four great doctors of the Church. Latimer replied with vigour; others ranged themselves on one side or the other, and there was general battle in the University; but the King's Almoner soon intervened with a letter commanding silence on both sides till the King's pleasure was further declared. The King's good-will to Latimer was due, as the letter indicated, to the understanding that Latimer "favoured the King's cause" in the question of divorce from Katherine of Arragon.

In March, 1530, Latimer was called to preach before Henry VIII., at Windsor. The King then made Latimer his chaplain, and in the following year gave him the rectory of West Kington, in Wiltshire. The new rector, soon accused of heresy, was summoned before the Bishop of London and before Convocation; was excommunicated and imprisoned, and absolved by special request of the King. When Cranmer became Archbishop of Canterbury, Latimer returned into royal favour, and preached before the King on Wednesdays in Lent. In 1535, when an Italian nominee of the Pope's was deprived of the Bishopric of Worcester, Latimer was made his successor; but resigned in 1539, when the King, having virtually made himself Pope, dictated to a tractable parliament enforcement of old doctrines by an Act for Abolishing Diversity of Opinion. From that time until the death of Henry VIII. Latimer was in disgrace.

The accession of Edward VI. brought him again to the front, and the Sermon on the Plough, in this volume, is a famous example of his use of his power under Edward VI., as the greatest preacher of his time, in forwarding the Reformation of the Church, and of the lives of those who professed and called themselves Christians. The rest of his story will be associated in another volume of this Library with a collection of his later sermons. H. M.

SERMONS ON THE CARD.

THE TENOR AND EFFECT OF CERTAIN SERMONS MADE BY MASTER LATIMER IN CAMBRIDGE, ABOUT THE YEAR OF OUR LORD 1529.

Tu quis es? Which words are as much to say in English, "Who art thou?" These be the words of the Pharisees, which were sent by the Jews unto St. John Baptist in the wilderness, to have knowledge of him who he was: which words they spake unto him of an evil intent, thinking that he would have taken on him to be Christ, and so they would have had him done with their good wills, because they knew that he was more carnal, and given to their laws, than Christ indeed should be, as they perceived by their old prophecies; and also, because they marvelled much of his great doctrine, preaching, and baptizing, they were in doubt whether he was Christ or not: wherefore they said unto him, "Who art thou?" Then answered St. John, and confessed that he was not Christ.

Now here is to be noted the great and prudent answer of St. John Baptist unto the Pharisees, that when they required of him who he was, he would not directly answer of himself what he was himself, but he said he was not Christ: by the which saying he thought to put the Jews and Pharisees out of their false opinion and belief towards him, in that they would have had him to exercise the office of Christ; and so declared further unto them of Christ, saying, "He is in the midst of you and amongst you, whom ye know not, whose latchet of his shoe I am not worthy to unloose, or undo." By this you may perceive that St. John spake much in the laud and praise of Christ his Master, professing himself to be in no wise like unto him. So likewise it shall be necessary unto all men and women of this world, not to ascribe unto themselves any goodness of themselves, but all unto our Lord God, as shall appear hereafter, when this question aforesaid, "Who art thou?" shall be moved unto them: not as the Pharisees did unto St. John, of an evil purpose, but of a good and simple mind, as may appear hereafter.

¶ Now then, according to the preacher's mind, let every man and woman, of a good and simple mind, contrary to the Pharisees' intent, ask this question, "Who art thou?" This question must be moved to themselves, what they be of themselves, on this fashion: "What art thou of thy only and natural generation between father and mother, when thou camest into this world? What substance, what virtue, what goodness art thou of, by thyself?" Which question if thou rehearse oftentimes unto thyself, thou shalt well perceive and understand how thou shalt make answer unto it; which must be made on this wise: I am of myself, and by myself, coming from my natural father and mother, the child of the ire and indignation of God, the true inheritor of hell, a lump of sin, and working nothing of myself but all towards hell, except I have better help of another than I have of myself. Now we may see in what state we enter into this world, that we be of ourselves the true and just inheritors of hell, the children of the ire and indignation of Christ, working all towards hell, whereby we deserve of ourselves perpetual damnation, by the right judgment of God, and the true claim of ourselves; which unthrifty state that we be born unto is come unto us for our own deserts, as proveth well this example following:

Let it be admitted for the probation of this, that it might please the king's grace now being to accept into his favour a mean man, of a simple degree and birth, not born to any possession; whom the king's grace favoureth, not because this person hath of himself deserved any such favour, but that the king casteth this favour unto him of his own mere motion and fantasy: and for because the king's grace will more declare his favour unto him, he giveth unto this said man a thousand pounds in lands, to him and his heirs, on this condition, that he shall take upon him to be the chief captain and defender of his town of Calais, and to be true and faithful to him in the custody of the same, against the Frenchmen especially, above all other enemies.

This man taketh on him this charge, promising his fidelity thereunto. It chanceth in process of time, that by the singular acquaintance and frequent familiarity of this captain with the Frenchmen, these Frenchmen give unto the said captain of Calais a great sum of money, so that he will but be content and agreeable that they may enter into the said town of Calais by force of arms; and so thereby possess the same unto the crown of France. Upon this agreement the Frenchmen do invade the said town of Calais, alonely by the negligence of this captain.

Now the king's grace, hearing of this invasion, cometh with a great puissance to defend this his said town, and so by good policy of war overcometh the said Frenchmen, and entereth again into his said town of Calais. Then he, being desirous to know how these enemies of his came thither, maketh profound search and inquiry by whom this treason was conspired. By this search it was known and found his own captain to be the very author and the beginner of the betraying of it. The king, seeing the great infidelity of this person, dischargeth this man of his office, and taketh from him and from his heirs this thousand pounds of possessions. Think you not that the king doth use justice unto him, and all his posterity and heirs? Yes, truly: the said captain cannot deny himself but that he had true justice, considering how unfaithfully he behaved him to his prince, contrary to his own fidelity and promise. So likewise it was of our first father Adam. He had given unto him the spirit of science and knowledge, to work all goodness therewith: this said spirit was not given alonely unto him, but unto all his heirs and posterity. He had also delivered him the town of Calais, that is to say, paradise in earth, the most strong and fairest town in the world, to be in his custody. He nevertheless, by the instigation of these Frenchmen, that is to say, the temptation of the fiend, did obey unto their desire; and so he brake his promise and fidelity, the commandment of the everlasting King his master, in eating of the apple by him inhibited.

Now then the King, seeing this great treason in his captain, deposed him of the thousand pounds of possessions, that is to say, from everlasting life in glory, and all his heirs and posterity: for likewise as he had the spirit of science and knowledge, for him and his heirs; so in like manner, when he lost the same, his heirs also lost it by him and in him. So now this example proveth, that by our father Adam we had once in him the very inheritance of everlasting joy; and by him, and in him, again we lost the same.

The heirs of the captain of Calais could not by any manner of claim ask of the king the right and title of their father in the thousand pounds of possessions, by reason the king might answer and say unto them, that although their father deserved not of himself to enjoy so great possessions, yet he deserved by himself to lose them, and greater, committing so high treason, as he did, against his prince's commandments; whereby he had no wrong to lose his title, but was unworthy to have the same, and had therein true justice. Let not you think, which be his heirs, that if he had justice to lose his possessions, you have wrong to lose the same. In the same manner it may be answered unto all men and women now being, that if our father Adam had true justice to be excluded from his possession of everlasting glory in paradise, let us not think the contrary that be his heirs, but that we have no wrong in losing also the same; yea, we have true justice and right. Then in what miserable estate we be, that of the right and just title of our own deserts have lost the everlasting joy, and claim of ourselves to be true inheritors of hell! For he that committeth deadly sin willingly, bindeth himself to be inheritor of everlasting pain: and so did our forefather Adam willingly eat of the apple forbidden. Wherefore he was cast out of the everlasting joy in paradise into this corrupt world, amongst all vileness, whereby of himself he was not worthy to do any thing laudable or pleasant to God, evermore bound to corrupt affections and beastly appetites, transformed into the most uncleanest and variablest nature that was made under heaven; of whose seed and disposition all the world is lineally descended, insomuch that this evil nature is so fused and shed from one into another, that at this day there is no man nor woman living that can of themselves wash away this abominable vileness: and so we must needs grant of ourselves to be in like displeasure unto God, as our forefather Adam was. By reason hereof, as I said, we be of ourselves the very children of the indignation and vengeance of God, the true inheritors of hell, and working all towards hell: which is the answer to this question, made to every man and woman, by themselves, "Who art thou?"

And now, the world standing in this damnable state, cometh in the occasion of the incarnation of Christ. The Father in heaven, perceiving the frail nature of man, that he, by himself and of himself, could do nothing for himself, by his prudent wisdom sent down the second person in Trinity, his Son Jesus Christ, to declare unto man his pleasure and commandment: and so, at the Father's will, Christ took on him human nature, being willing to deliver man out of this miserable way, and was content to suffer cruel passion in shedding his blood for all mankind; and so left behind for our safeguard laws and ordinances, to keep us always in the right path unto everlasting life, as the evangelists, the sacraments, the commandments, and so forth: which, if we do keep and observe according to our profession, we shall answer better unto this question, "Who art thou?" than we did before. For before thou didst enter into the sacrament of baptism, thou wert but a natural man, a natural woman; as I might say, a man, a woman: but after thou takest on thee Christ's religion, thou hast a longer name; for then thou art a christian man, a christian woman. Now then, seeing thou art a christian man, what shall be thy answer of this question, "Who art thou?"

The answer of this question is, when I ask it unto myself, I must say that I am a christian man, a christian woman, the child of everlasting joy, through the merits of the bitter passion of Christ. This is a joyful answer. Here we may see how much we be bound and in danger unto God, that hath revived us from death to life, and saved us that were damned: which great benefit we cannot well consider, unless we do remember what we were of ourselves before we meddled with him or his laws; and the more we know our feeble nature, and set less by it, the more we shall conceive and know in our hearts what God hath done for us; and the more we know what God hath done for us, the less we shall set by ourselves, and the more we shall love and please God: so that in no condition we shall either know ourselves or God, except we do utterly confess ourselves to be mere vileness and corruption. Well, now it is come unto this point, that we be christian men, christian women, I pray you what doth Christ require of a christian man, or of a christian woman? Christ requireth nothing else of a christian man or woman, but that they will observe his rule: for likewise as he is a good Augustine friar that keepeth well St. Augustine's rule, so is he a good christian man that keepeth well Christ's rule.

Now then, what is Christ's rule? Christ's rule consisteth in many things, as in the commandments, and the works of mercy, and so forth. And for because I cannot declare Christ's rule unto you at one time, as it ought to be done, I will apply myself according to your custom at this time of Christmas: I will, as I said, declare unto you Christ's rule, but that shall be in Christ's cards. And whereas you are wont to celebrate Christmas in playing at cards, I intend, by God's grace, to deal unto you Christ's cards, wherein you shall perceive Christ's rule. The game that we will play at shall be called the triumph, which, if it be well played at, he that dealeth shall win;

the players shall likewise win; and the standers and lookers upon shall do the same; insomuch that there is no man that is willing to play at this triumph with these cards, but they shall be all winners, and no losers.

Let therefore every christian man and woman play at these cards, that they may have and obtain the triumph: you must mark also that the triumph must apply to fetch home unto him all the other cards, whatsoever suit they be of. Now then, take ye this first card, which must appear and be shewed unto you as followeth: you have heard what was spoken to men of the old law, "Thou shalt not kill; whosoever shall kill shall be in danger of judgment: but I say unto you" of the new law, saith Christ, "that whosoever is angry with his neighbour, shall be in danger of judgment; and whosoever shall say unto his neighbour, 'Raca,' that is to say, brainless," or any other like word of rebuking, "shall be in danger of council; and whosoever shall say unto his neighbour, 'Fool,' shall be in danger of hell-fire." This card was made and spoken by Christ, as appeareth in the fifth chapter of St. Matthew.

Now it must be noted, that whosoever shall play with this card, must first, before they play with it, know the strength and virtue of the same: wherefore you must well note and mark terms, how they be spoken, and to what purpose. Let us therefore read it once or twice, that we may be the better acquainted with it.

Now behold and see, this card is divided into four parts: the first part is one of the commandments that was given unto Moses in the old law, before the coming of Christ; which commandment we of the new law be bound to observe and keep, and it is one of our commandments. The other three parts spoken by Christ be nothing else but expositions unto the first part of this commandment: for in very effect all these four parts be but one commandment, that is to say, "Thou shalt not kill." Yet nevertheless, the last three parts do shew unto thee how many ways thou mayest kill thy neighbour contrary to this commandment: yet, for all Christ's exposition in the three last parts of this card, the terms be not open enough to thee that dost read and hear them spoken. No doubt, the Jews understood Christ well enough, when he spake to them these three last sentences; for he spake unto them in their own natural terms and tongue. Wherefore, seeing that these terms were natural terms of the Jews, it shall be necessary to expound them, and compare them unto some like terms of our natural speech, that we, in like manner, may understand Christ as well as the Jews did. We will begin first with the first part of this card, and then after, with the other three parts. You must therefore understand that the Jews and the Pharisees of the old law, to whom this first part, this commandment, "Thou shalt not kill," was spoken, thought it sufficient and enough for their discharge, not to kill with any manner of material weapon, as sword, dagger, or with any such weapon; and they thought it no great fault whatsoever they said or did by their neighbours, so that they did not harm or meddle with their corporal bodies: which was a false opinion in them, as prove well the three last other sentences following the first part of this card.

Now, as touching the three other sentences, you must note and take heed, what difference is between these three manner of offences: to be angry with your neighbour; to call your neighbour "brainless," or any such word of disdain; or to call your neighbour "fool." Whether these three manner of offences be of themselves more grievous one than the other, it is to be opened unto you. Truly, as they be of themselves divers offences, so they kill diversly, one more than the other; as you shall perceive by the first of these three, and so forth. A man which conceiveth against his neighbour or brother ire or wrath in his mind, by some manner of occasion given unto him, although he be angry in his mind against his said neighbour, he will peradventure express his ire by no manner of sign, either in word or deed: yet, nevertheless, he offendeth against God, and breaketh this commandment in killing his own soul; and is therefore "in danger of judgment."

Now, to the second part of these three: That man that is moved with ire against his neighbour, and in his ire calleth his neighbour "brainless," or some other like word of displeasure; as a man might say in a fury, "I shall handle thee well enough;" which words and countenances do more represent and declare ire to be in this man, than in him that was but angry, and spake no manner of word nor shewed any countenance to declare his ire. Wherefore as he that so declareth his ire either by word or countenance offendeth more against God, so he both killeth his own soul, and doth that in him is to kill his neighbour's soul in moving him unto ire, wherein he is faulty himself; and so this man is "in danger of council."

Now to the third offence, and last of these three: That man that calleth his neighbour "fool," doth more declare his angry mind toward him, than he that called his neighbour but "brainless," or any such words moving ire: for to call a man "fool," that word representeth more envy in a man than "brainless" doth. Wherefore he doth most offend, because he doth most earnestly with such words express his ire, and so he is "in danger of hell-fire."

Wherefore you may understand now, these three parts of this card be three offences, and that one is more grievous to God than the other, and that one killeth more the soul of man than the other.

Now peradventure there be some that will marvel, that Christ did not declare this commandment by some greater faults of ire, than by these which seem but small faults, as to be angry and speak nothing of it, to declare it and to call a man "brainless," and to call his neighbour "fool:" truly these be the smallest and the least faults that belong to ire, or to killing in ire. Therefore beware how you offend in any kind of ire: seeing that the smallest be damnable to offend in, see that you offend not in the greatest. For Christ thought, if he might bring you from the smallest manner of faults, and give you warning to avoid the least, he reckoned you would not offend in the greatest and worst, as to call your neighbour thief, whoreson, whore, drab, and so forth, into more blasphemous names; which offences must needs have punishment in hell, considering how that Christ hath appointed these three small faults to have three degrees of punishment in hell, as appeareth by these three terms, judgment, council, and hell-fire. These three terms do signify nothing else but three divers punishments in hell, according to the offences. Judgment is less in degree than council, therefore it signifieth a lesser pain in hell, and it is ordained for him that is angry in his mind with his neighbour, and doth express his malice neither by word nor countenance: council is a less degree in hell than hell-fire, and is a greater degree in hell than judgment; and it is ordained for him that calleth his neighbour "brainless," or any such word, that declareth his ire and malice: wherefore it is more pain than judgment. Hell-fire is more pain in hell than council or judgment, and it is ordained for him that calleth his neighbour " fool," by reason that in calling his neighbour " fool," he declareth more his malice, in that it is an earnest word of ire : wherefore hell-fire is appointed for it; that is, the most pain of the three punishments.

Now you have heard, that to these divers offences of ire and killing be appointed punishments according to their degrees : for look as the offence is, so shall the pain be : if the offence be great, the pain shall be according ; if it be less, there shall be less pain for it. I would not now that you should think, because that here are but three degrees of punishment spoken of, that there be no more in hell. No doubt Christ spake of no more here but of these three degrees of punishment, thinking they were sufficient, enough for example, whereby we might understand that there be as divers and many pains as there be offences : and so by these three offences, and these three punishments, all other offences and punishments may be compared with another. Yet I would satisfy your minds further in these three terms, of " judgment, council, and hell-fire." Whereas you might say, What was the cause that Christ declared more the pains of hell by these terms than by any other terms? I told you afore that he knew well to whom he spake them. These terms were natural and well known amongst the Jews and the Pharisees: wherefore Christ taught them with their own terms, to the intent they might understand the better his doctrine. And these terms may be likened unto three terms which we have common and usual amongst us, that is to say, the sessions of inquirance, the sessions of deliverance, and the execution-day. Sessions of inquirance is like unto judgment; for when sessions of inquiry is, then the judges cause twelve men to give verdict of the felon's crime, whereby he shall be judged to be indicted: sessions of deliverance is much like council; for at sessions of deliverance the judges go among themselves to council, to determine sentence against the felon: execution-day is to be compared unto hell-fire; for the Jews had amongst themselves a place of execution, named "hell-fire:"

and surely when a man goeth to his death, it is the greatest pain in this world. Wherefore you may see that there are degrees in these our terms, as there be in those terms.

These evil-disposed affections and sensualities in us are always contrary to the rule of our salvation. What shall we do now or imagine to thrust down these Turks and to subdue them? It is a great ignominy and shame for a christian man to be bond and subject unto a Turk: nay, it shall not be so; we will first cast a trump in their way, and play with them at cards, who shall have the better. Let us play therefore on this fashion with this card. Whensoever it shall happen the foul passions and Turks to rise in our stomachs against our brother or neighbour, either for unkind words, injuries, or wrongs, which they have done unto us, contrary unto our mind; straightways let us call unto our remembrance, and speak this question unto ourselves, "Who art thou?" The answer is, "I am a christian man." Then further we must say to ourselves, "What requireth Christ of a christian man?" Now turn up your trump, your heart (hearts is trump, as I said before), and cast your trump, your heart, on this card; and upon this card you shall learn what Christ requireth of a christian man—not to be angry, ne moved to ire against his neighbour, in mind, countenance, nor other ways, by word or deed. Then take up this card with your heart, and lay them together: that done, you have won the game of the Turk, whereby you have defaced and overcome him by true and lawful play. But, alas for pity! the Rhodes are won and overcome by these false Turks; the strong castle Faith is decayed, so that I fear it is almost impossible to win it again.

The great occasion of the loss of this Rhodes is by reason that christian men do so daily kill their own nation, that the very true number of Christianity is decayed; which murder and killing one of another is increased specially two ways, to the utter undoing of Christendom, that is to say, by example and silence. By example, as thus: when the father, the mother, the lord, the lady, the master, the dame, be themselves overcome by these Turks, they be continual swearers, avouterers, disposers to malice, never in patience, and so forth in all other vices : think you not, when the father, the mother, the master, the dame, be disposed unto vice or impatience, but that their children and servants shall incline and be disposed to the same? No doubt, as the child shall take disposition natural of the father and mother, so shall the servants apply unto the vices of their masters and dames: if the heads be false in their faculties and crafts, it is no marvel if the children, servants, and apprentices do joy therein. This is a great and shameful manner of killing christian men, that the fathers, the mothers, the masters, and the dames shall not alonely kill themselves, but all theirs, and all that belongeth unto them : and so this way is a great number of christian lineage murdered and spoiled.

The second manner of killing is silence. By silence also is a great number of christian men slain; which is on this fashion : although that the father and mother, master and dame, of themselves be well disposed to live according to the law of God, yet they may kill their children and servants in suffering them to do evil before their own faces, and do not use due correction according unto their offences. The master seeth his servant or apprentice take more of his neighbour than the king's laws, or the order of his faculty, doth admit him; or that he suffereth him to take more of his neighbour than he himself would be content to pay, if he were in like condition: thus doing, I say, such men kill willingly their children and servants, and shall go to hell for so doing; but also their fathers and mothers, masters and dames, shall bear them company for so suffering them.

Wherefore I exhort all true christian men and women to give good example unto your children and servants, and suffer not them by silence to offend. Every man must be in his own house, according to St. Augustine's mind, a bishop, not alonely giving good ensample, but teaching according to it, rebuking and punishing vice; not suffering your children and servants to forget the laws of God. You ought to see them have their belief, to know the commandments of God, to keep their holy-days, not to lose their time in idleness: if they do so, you shall all suffer pain for it, if God be true of his saying, as there is no doubt thereof. And so you may perceive that there be many a one that breaketh this card, "Thou shalt not kill," and playeth therewith oftentime at the blind trump, whereby they be no winners, but great losers. But who be those now-a-days that can clear themselves of these manifest murders used to their children and servants? I think not the contrary, but that many have these two ways slain their own children unto their damnation; unless the great mercy of God were ready to help them when they repent there-for.

Wherefore, considering that we be so prone and ready to continue in sin, let us cast down ourselves with **Mary Magdalene**; and the more we bow down with her toward Christ's feet, the more we shall be afraid to rise again in sin; and the more we know and submit ourselves, the more we shall be forgiven; and the less we know and submit ourselves, the less we shall be forgiven; as appeareth by this example following:

Christ, when he was in this world, amongst the Jews and Pharisees, there was a great Pharisee whose name was Simon: this Pharisee desired Christ on a time to dine with him, thinking in himself that he was able and worthy to give Christ a dinner. Christ refused not his dinner, but came unto him. In time of their dinner it chanced there came into the house a great and a common sinner named Mary Magdalene. As soon as she perceived Christ, she cast herself down, and called unto her remembrance what she was of herself, and how greatly she had offended God; whereby she conceived in Christ great love, and so came near unto him, and washed his feet with bitter tears, and shed upon his head precious ointment, thinking that by him she should be delivered from her sins. This great and proud Pharisee, seeing that Christ did accept her oblation in the best part, had great indignation against this woman, and said to himself, "If this man Christ were a holy prophet, as he is taken for, he would not suffer this sinner to come so nigh him." Christ, understanding the naughty mind of this Pharisee, said unto him, "Simon, I have somewhat to say unto thee." "Say what you please," quod the Pharisee. Then said Christ, "I pray thee, tell me this: If there be a man to whom is owing twenty pound by one, and forty by another, this man to whom this money is owing, perceiving these two men be not able to pay him, he forgiveth them both: which of these two debtors ought to love this man most?" The Pharisee said, "That man ought to love him best, that had most forgiven him." "Likewise," said Christ, "it is by this woman: she hath loved me most, therefore most is forgiven her; she hath known her sins most, whereby she hath most loved me. And thou hast least loved me, because thou hast least known thy sins: therefore, because thou hast least known thine offences, thou art least forgiven." So this proud Pharisee had an answer to delay his pride. And think you not, but that there be amongst us a great number of these proud Pharisees, which think themselves worthy to bid Christ to dinner; which will perk, and presume to sit by Christ in the church, and have a disdain of this poor woman Magdalene, their poor neighbour, with a high, disdainous, and solemn countenance? And being always desirous to climb highest in the church, reckoning themselves more worthy to sit there than another, I fear me poor Magdalene under the board, and in the belfry, hath more forgiven of Christ than they have: for it is like that those Pharisees do less know themselves and their offences, whereby they less love God, and so they be less forgiven.

I would to God we would follow this example, and be like unto Magdalene. I doubt not but we be all Magdalenes in falling into sin and in offending: but we be not again Magdalenes in knowing ourselves, and in rising from sin. If we be the true Magdalenes, we should be as willing to forsake our sin and rise from sin, as we were willing to commit sin and to continue in it; and we then should know ourselves best, and make more perfect answer than ever we did unto this question, "Who art thou?" to the which we might answer, that we be true christian men and women: and then, I say, you should understand, and know how you ought to play at this card, "Thou shalt not kill," without any interruption of your deadly enemies the Turks; and so triumph at the last, by winning everlasting life in glory. Amen.

ANOTHER SERMON OF M. LATIMER, CONCERNING THE SAME MATTER.

Now you have heard what is meant by this first card, and how you ought to play with it, I purpose again to deal unto you another card, almost of the same suit; for they be of so nigh affinity, that one cannot be well played without the other. The first card declared, that you should not kill, which might be done divers ways; as being angry with your neighbour, in mind, in countenance, in word, or deed: it declared also, how you should subdue the passions of ire, and so clear evermore yourselves from them. And whereas this first card doth kill in you these stubborn Turks of ire; this second card will not only they should be mortified in you, but that you yourselves shall cause them to be likewise mortified in your neighbour, if that your said neighbour hath been through your occasion moved unto ire, either in countenance, word, or deed. Now let us hear therefore the tenor of this card: "When thou makest thine oblation at mine altar, and there dost remember that thy neighbour hath any thing against thee, lay down there thy oblation, and go first and reconcile thy neighbour, and then come and offer thy oblation."

This card was spoken by Christ, as testifieth St. Matthew in his fifth chapter, against all such as do presume to come unto the church to make oblation unto God either by prayer, or any other deed of charity, not having their neighbours reconciled. Reconciling is as much to say as to restore thy neighbour unto charity, which by thy words or deeds is moved against thee: then, if so be it that thou hast spoken to or by thy neighbour, whereby he is moved to ire or wrath, thou must lay down thy oblation. Oblations be prayers, alms-deeds, or any work of charity: these be all called oblations to God. Lay down therefore thine oblation; begin to do none of these foresaid works before thou goest unto thy neighbour, and confess thy fault unto him; declaring thy mind, that if thou hast offended him, thou art glad and willing to make him amends, as far forth as thy words and substance will extend, requiring him not to take it at the worst: thou art sorry in thy mind, that thou shouldest be occasion of his offending.

"What manner of card is this?" will some say: "Why, what have I to do with my neighbour's or brother's malice?" As Cain said, "Have I the keeping of my brother? or shall I answer for him and for his faults? This were no reason—As for myself, I thank God I owe no man malice nor displeasure: if others owe me any, at their own peril be it. Let every man answer for himself!" Nay, sir, not so, as you may understand by this card; for it saith, "If thy neighbour hath anything, any malice against thee, through thine occasion, lay even down (saith Christ) thine oblation: pray not to me; do no good deeds for me; but go first unto thy neighbour, and bring him again unto my flock, which hath forsaken the same through thy naughty words, mocks, scorns, or disdainous countenance, and so forth; and then come and offer thine oblation; then do thy devotion; then do thy alms-deeds; then pray, if thou wilt have me hear thee."

"O good Lord! this is a hard reckoning, that I must go and seek him out that is offended with me, before I pray or do any good deed. I cannot go unto him. Peradventure he is a hundred miles from me, beyond the seas; or else I cannot tell where: if he were here nigh, I would with all my heart go unto him." This is a lawful excuse before God on this fashion, that thou wouldest in thy heart be glad to reconcile thy neighbour, if he were present; and that thou thinkest in thy heart, whensoever thou shalt meet with him, to go unto him, and require him charitably to forgive thee; and so never intend to come from him, until the time that you both depart one from the other true brethren in Christ.

Yet, peradventure, there be some in the world that be so devilish, and so hard-hearted, that they will not apply in any condition unto charity. For all that, do what lieth in thee, by all charitable means, to bring him to unity. If he will in no wise apply thereunto, thou mayest be sorrowful in thy heart, that by thine occasion that man or woman continueth in such a damnable state. This notwithstanding, if thou do the best that lieth in thee to reconcile him, according to some doctors' mind, thou art discharged towards God. Nevertheless St. Augustine doubteth in this case, whether thy oblations, prayers, or good deeds, shall avail thee before God, or no, until thy neighbour come again to good state, whom thou hast brought out of the way. Doth this noble doctor doubt therein?

What aileth us to be so bold, and count it but a small fault, or none, to bring our neighbour out of patience for every trifle that standeth not with our mind? You may see what a grievous thing this is, to bring another man out of patience, that peradventure you cannot bring in again with all the goods that you have: for surely, after the opinion of great wise men, friendship once broken will be never well made whole again. Wherefore you shall hear what Christ saith unto such persons. Saith Christ, "I came down into this world, and so took on me bitter passion for man's sake, by the merits whereof I intended to make unity and peace in mankind, to make man brother unto me, and so to expel the dominion of Satan, the devil, which worketh nothing else but dissension: and yet now there be a great number of you, that have professed my name, and say you be christian men, which do rebel against my purpose and mind. I go about to make my fold: you go about to break the same, and kill my flock." "How darest thou," saith Christ, "presume to come unto my altar, unto my church, or into my presence, to make oblation unto me, that takest on thee to spoil my lambs? I go about like a good shepherd to gather them together; and thou dost the contrary, evermore ready to divide and lose them. Who made thee so bold to meddle with my silly beasts, which I bought so dearly with my precious blood? I warn thee out of my sight, come not in my presence: I refuse thee and all thy works, except thou go and bring home again my lambs which thou hast lost. Wherefore, if thou thyself intend to be one of mine, lay even down by and by thine oblation, and come no further toward mine altar; but go and seek them without any questions, as it becometh a true and faithful servant."

A true and faithful servant, whensoever his master commandeth him to do any thing, he maketh no stops nor questions, but goeth forth with a good mind: and it is not unlike he, continuing in such a good mind and will, shall well overcome all dangers and stops, whatsoever betide him in his journey, and bring to pass effectually his master's will and pleasure On the contrary, a slothful servant, when his master commandeth him to do any thing, by and by he will ask questions, "Where?" "When?" "Which way?" and so forth; and so he putteth every thing in doubt, that although both his errand and way be never so plain, yet by his untoward and slothful behaviour his master's commandment is either undone quite, or else so done that it shall stand to no good purpose. Go now forth with the good servant, and ask no such questions, and put no doubts. Be not ashamed to do thy Master's and Lord's will and commandment. Go, as I said, unto thy neighbour that is offended by thee, and reconcile him (as is afore said) whom thou hast lost by thy unkind words, by thy scorns, mocks, and other disdainous words and behaviours; and be not nice to ask of him the cause why he is displeased with thee: require of him charitably to remit; and cease not till you both depart, one from the other, true brethren in Christ.

Do not, like the slothful servant, thy master's

message with cautels and doubts: come not to thy neighbour whom thou hast offended, and give him a pennyworth of ale, or a banquet, and so make him a fair countenance, thinking that by thy drink or dinner he will shew thee like countenance. I grant you may both laugh and make good cheer, and yet there may remain a bag of rusty malice, twenty years old, in thy neighbour's bosom. When he departeth from thee with a good countenance, thou thinkest all is well then. But now, I tell thee, it is worse than it was, for by such cloaked charity, where thou dost offend before Christ but once, thou hast offended twice herein: for now thou goest about to give Christ a mock, if he would take it of thee. Thou thinkest to blind thy master Christ's commandment. Beware, do not so, for at length he will overmatch thee, and take thee tardy whatsoever thou be; and so, as I said, it should be better for thee not to do his message on this fashion, for it will stand thee in no purpose. "What?" some will say, "I am sure he loveth me well enough: he speaketh fair to my face." Yet for all that thou mayest be deceived. It proveth not true love in a man, to speak fair. If he love thee with his mind and heart, he loveth thee with his eyes, with his tongue, with his feet, with his hands and his body; for all these parts of a man's body be obedient to the will and mind. He loveth thee with his eyes, that looketh cheerfully on thee, when thou meetest with him, and is glad to see thee prosper and do well. He loveth thee with his tongue, that speaketh well by thee behind thy back, or giveth thee good counsel. He loveth thee with his feet, that is willing to go to help thee out of trouble and business. He loveth thee with his hands, that will help thee in time of necessity, by giving some alms-deeds, or with any other occupation of the hand. He loveth thee with his body, that will labour with his body, or put his body in danger to do good for thee, or to deliver thee from adversity: and so forth, with the other members of his body. And if thy neighbour will do according to these sayings, then thou mayest think that he loveth thee well; and thou, in like wise, oughtest to declare and open thy love unto thy neighbour in like fashion, or else you be bound one to reconcile the other, till this perfect love be engendered amongst you.

It may fortune thou wilt say, "I am content to do the best for my neighbour that I can, saving myself harmless." I promise thee, Christ will not hear this excuse; for he himself suffered harm for our sakes, and for our salvation was put to extreme death. I wis, if it had pleased him, he might have saved us and never felt pain; but in suffering pains and death he did give us example, and teach us how we should do one for another, as he did for us all; for, as he saith himself, "he that will be mine, let him deny himself, and follow me, in bearing my cross and suffering my pains." Wherefore we must needs suffer pain with Christ to do our neighbour good, as well with the body and all his members, as with heart and mind.

Now I trust you wot what your card meaneth: let us see how that we can play with the same.

Whensoever it shall happen you to go and make your oblation unto God, ask of yourselves this question, "Who art thou?" The answer, as you know, is, "I am a christian man." Then you must again ask unto yourself, What Christ requireth of a christian man? By and by cast down your trump, your heart, and look first of one card, then of another. The first card telleth thee, thou shalt not kill, thou shalt not be angry, thou shalt not be out of patience. This done, thou shalt look if there be any more cards to take up; and if thou look well, thou shalt see another card of the same suit, wherein thou shalt know that thou art bound to reconcile thy neighbour. Then cast thy trump upon them both, and gather them all three together, and do according to the virtue of thy cards; and surely thou shalt not lose. Thou shalt first kill the great Turks, and discomfort and thrust them down. Thou shalt again fetch home Christ's sheep that thou hast lost; whereby thou mayest go both patiently and with a quiet mind unto the church, and make thy oblation unto

God; and then, without doubt, he will hear thee.

But yet Christ will not accept our oblation (although we be in patience, and have reconciled our neighbour), if that our oblation be made of another man's substance; but it must be our own. See therefore that thou hast gotten thy goods according to the laws of God and of thy prince. For if thou gettest thy goods by polling and extortion, or by any other unlawful ways, then, if thou offer a thousand pound of it, it will stand thee in no good effect; for it is not thine. In this point a great number of executors do offend; for when they be made rich by other men's goods, then they will take upon them to build churches, to give ornaments to God and his altar, to gild saints, and to do many good works therewith; but it shall be all in their own name, and for their own glory. Wherefore, saith Christ, they have in this world their reward; and so their oblations be not their own, nor be they acceptable before God.

Another way God will refuse thy voluntary oblation, as thus : if so be it that thou hast gotten never so truly thy goods, according both to the laws of God and man, and hast with the same goods not relieved thy poor neighbour, when thou hast seen him hungry, thirsty, and naked, he will not take thy oblation when thou shalt offer the same, because he will say unto thee, "When I was hungry, thou gavest me no meat; when I was thirsty, thou gavest me no drink; and when I was naked, thou didst not clothe me. Wherefore I will not take thy oblation, because it is none of thine. I left it thee to relieve thy poor neighbours, and thou hast not therein done according unto this my commandment, *Misericordiam volo, et non sacrificium ;* I had rather have mercy done, than sacrifice or oblation. Wherefore until thou dost the one more than the other, I will not accept thine oblation."

Evermore bestow the greatest part of thy goods in works of mercy, and the less part in voluntary works. Voluntary works be called all manner of offering in the church, except your four offering-days, and your tithes : setting up candles, gilding and painting, building of churches, giving of ornaments, going on pilgrimages, making of highways, and such other, be called voluntary works; which works be of themselves marvellous good, and convenient to be done. Necessary works, and works of mercy, are called the commandments, the four offering-days, your tithes, and such other that belong to the commandments; and works of mercy consist in relieving and visiting thy poor neighbours. Now then, if men be so foolish of themselves, that they will bestow the most part of their goods in voluntary works, which they be not bound to keep, but willingly and by their devotion; and leave the necessary works undone, which they are bound to do; they and all their voluntary works are like to go unto everlasting damnation. And I promise you, if you build a hundred churches, give as much as you can make to gilding of saints, and honouring of the church; and if thou go as many pilgrimages as thy body can well suffer, and offer as great candles as oaks; if thou leave the works of mercy and the commandments undone, these works shall nothing avail thee. No doubt the voluntary works be good and ought to be done; but yet they must be so done, that by their occasion the necessary works and the works of mercy be not decayed and forgotten. If you will build a glorious church unto God, see first yourself to be in charity with your neighbours, and suffer not them to be offended by your works. Then, when ye come into your parish-church, you bring with you the holy temple of God; as St. Paul saith, "You yourselves be the very holy temples of God:" and Christ saith by his prophet, "In you will I rest, and intend to make my mansion and abiding-place." Again, if you list to gild and paint Christ in your churches, and honour him in vestments, see that before your eyes the poor people die not for lack of meat, drink, and clothing. Then do you deck the very true temple of God, and honour him in rich vestures that will never be worn, and so forth use yourselves according unto the commandments: and then, finally, set up your candles, and they will report what a glorious light remaineth in your hearts; for it is not fitting to see a dead man light candles. Then, I say, go your pilgrimages, build your material churches, do all your voluntary works; and they will then represent you unto God, and testify with you, that you have provided him a glorious place in your hearts. But beware, I say again, that you do not run so far in your voluntary works, that ye do quite forget your necessary works of mercy, which you are bound to keep: you must have ever a good respect unto the best and worthiest works toward God to be done first and with more efficacy, and the other to be done secondarily. Thus if you do, with the other that I have spoken of before, ye may come according to the tenor of your cards, and offer your oblations and prayers to our Lord Jesus Christ, who will both hear and accept them to your everlasting joy and glory: to the which he bring us, and all those whom he suffered death for. Amen.

A SERMON MADE BY M. HUGH LATIMER, AT THE TIME OF THE INSURRECTION IN THE NORTH, WHICH WAS IN THE TWENTY-SEVENTH YEAR OF THE REIGN OF KING HENRY THE EIGHTH, ANN. DOM. 1535. UPON THE EPISTLE READ IN THE CHURCH THE TWENTY-FIRST SUNDAY AFTER TRINITY SUNDAY, TAKEN OUT OF THE SIXTH CHAPTER OF THE EPISTLE OF ST. PAUL TO THE EPHESIANS.

¶ *Put on all the armour of God, that ye may stand, &c.*
[Ephes. vi. 10, et seq.]

SAINT PAUL, the holy apostle, writeth this epistle unto the Ephesians, that is, to the people of the city of Ephesus. He writeth generally, to them all; and in the former chapters he teacheth them severally how they should behave themselves, in every estate, one to another; how they should obey their rulers; how wives should behave themselves towards their husbands; children towards their parents; and servants towards their masters; and husbands, parents and masters should behave them, and love their wives, children, and servants; and generally each to love other.

Now cometh he forth and comforteth them, and teacheth them to be bold, and to play the men, and fight manfully. For they must fight with valiant warriors, as appeareth afterward in the text. And against they come to fight he comforteth them, saying, "My brethren." He calleth them brethren; for though he taught them before to be subject to kings and rulers, and to be obedient to their superiors, yet he teacheth them that in Christ we be all brethren, according to the saying in this same chapter, "God is no accepter of persons." "My brethren," saith he, "be ye comforted, be ye strong;" not trusting to yourselves; no, but be bold, and comforted "by our Lord, and by the power of his virtue:" not by your own virtue, for it is not of power to resist such assaults as he speaketh of hereafter. "Put on, or apparel you with, the armour of God." Armour is an apparel to clothe a man, and maketh him seemly and comely; setteth forth his body, and maketh him strong and bold in battle. And therefore Saint Paul exhorteth generally his brethren to be armed; and as the assaults be strong, and not small, so he giveth strong armour, and not small: "Put on," saith he, "the armour of God." He speaketh generally of armour, but afterwards he speaketh particularly of the parts of armour, where he saith, be armed complete, whole; be armed on every part with the armour of God; not borrowed, nor patched, but all godly. And as armour setteth forth a man's body, so this godly armour maketh us seemly in the sight of God, and acceptable in his wars.

Be ye therefore "armed at all points with the armour of God, that ye may stand strongly against the assaults of the devil." "That ye may stand," saith he. Ye must stand in this battle, and not sit, nor lie along; for he that lieth is trodden under foot of his enemy. We may not sit, that is, not rest in sin, or lie along in sluggishness of sin; but continually fight against our enemy, and under our great Captain and Sovereign Lord Jesus Christ, and in his quarrel, armed with the armour of God, that we may be strong. We cannot be strong unless we be armed of God. We have no power of ourselves to stand against the assaults of the devil. There St. Paul teacheth what our battle is, and wherefore we must be thus armed.

For, saith he, " we have not wrestling or strife against flesh and blood : " which may be understood, against certain sins, which come of the flesh only; but let us take it as it standeth, "against flesh and blood," that is, against any corporal man, which is but a weak thing in comparison, and with one stroke destroyed or slain : but we have to do with strong, mighty princes and potentates ; that mighty prince, that great conqueror of this world, the devil, yea a conqueror: for though our Saviour Jesus Christ conquered him and all his, by suffering his blessed passion, yet is he a great conqueror in this world, and reigneth over a great multitude of his own, and maketh continual conflicts and assaults against the rest, to subdue them also under his power ; which, if they be armed after St. Paul's teaching, shall stand strongly against his assaults.

"Our battle," saith St. Paul, "is against princes, potestates," that is, against devils: for, after the common opinion, there fell from heaven of every order of angels, as of potentates. He saith also, "against worldly rulers of these darknesses:" for, as doctors do write, the spirits that fell with Lucifer have their being in *aëre caliginoso*, the air, in darkness, and the rulers of this world, by God's sufferance, to hurt, vex and assault them that live upon the earth. For their nature is, as they be damned, to desire to draw all mankind unto like damnation; such is their malice. And though they hang in the air, or fall in a garden or other pleasant place, yet have they continually their pain upon their backs. Against these we wrestle, and "against spiritual wickedness in *cœlestibus*," that is, in the air; or we fight against spiritual wickedness in heavenly things.

Think you not that this our enemy, this prince with all his potentates, hath great and sore assaults to lay against our armour? Yea, he is a crafty warrior, and also of great power in this world; he hath great ordnance and artillery; he hath great pieces of ordnance, as mighty kings and emperors, to shoot against God's people, to persecute or kill them; Nero, the great tyrant, who slew Paul, and divers other. Yea, what great pieces hath he had of bishops of Rome, which have destroyed whole cities and countries, and have slain and burnt many! What great guns were those!

Yea, he hath also less ordnance evil enough, (they may be called *serpentines;*) some bishops in divers countries, and here in England, which he hath shot at some good christian men, that they have been blown to ashes. So can this great captain, the devil, shoot his ordnance. He hath yet less ordnance, for he hath of all sorts to shoot at good christian men; he hath hand-guns and bows, which do much hurt, but not so much as the great ordnance. These be accusers, promoters, and slanderers; they be evil ordnance, shrewd hand-guns, and bows; they put a man to great displeasure; oftentimes death cometh upon that shot. For these things, saith the text, " take the armour of God." Against the great captains, the devils, and against their artillery, their ministers, there can nothing defend us but the armour of God.

"Take therefore this armour," saith the text, "that ye may resist in the evil day, and in all things stand perfectly, or be perfectly strong." This evil day is not so called here, because any day or time is evil; for God made every day good, and all days be good: but St. Paul calleth it the "evil day," because of the misfortune that chanceth or cometh in that day. As we have a common saying, "I have had an evil day, and an evil night," because of the heaviness or evil that hath happened; so saith Paul, "that ye may resist in the evil day:" that is, when your great adversary hath compassed you round about with his potestates and rulers, and with his artillery, so that you be almost overcome, then, if you have the armour of God, you shall be strong, and need not to fear his assaults.

St. Paul hath spoken of this armour of God generally, and now declareth the parts and pieces of armour; and teacheth them how to apparel every part of the body with this armour. He beginneth yet again, saying, "Be strong, having your reins, or your loins girded about." Some men of war use to have about their loins an apron or girdle of mail, gird fast for the safeguard of the nether part of their body. So St. Paul would we should gird our loins, which betokeneth lechery or other sinfulness, with a girdle, which is to be taken for a restraint or continence from such vices. In "truth," or "truly gird:" it may not be feigned, or falsely girt, but in verity and truth. There be many bachelors, as yet men unmarried, which seem to be girt with the girdle of continence, and yet it is not in truth, it is but feignedly. And some religious persons make a profession of continence or chastity, and yet not in truth, their hearts be not truly chaste. Such feigned girding of the loins cannot make a man strong to resist the assaults of the great captain or enemy in the evil day. Yet some get them girdles with great knots, as though they would be surely girt, and as though they would break the devil's head with their knotted girdles. Nay, he will not be so overcome: it is no knot of an hempton girdle that he feareth; that is no piece of harness of the armour of God, which may resist the assault in the evil day; it is but feigned gear; it must be in the heart, &c.

"And be ye apparelled or clothed," saith Paul, "with the habergeon or coat-armour of justice, that is, righteousness." Let your body be clothed in the armour of righteousness: ye may do no wrong to any man, but live in righteousness; not clothed with any false quarrel or privy grudge. Ye must live rightly in God's law, following his commandments and doctrine, clothed righteously in his armour, and not in any feigned armour, as in a friar's coat or cowl. For the assaults of the devil be crafty: to make us put our trust in such armour, he will feign himself to fly; but then we be most in jeopardy: for he can give us an after-clap when we least ween; that is, suddenly return unawares to us, and then he giveth us an after-clap that overthroweth us: this armour deceiveth us.

In like manner these men in the North country, they make pretence as though they were armed in

God's armour, gird in truth, and clothed in righteousness. I hear say they wear the cross and the wounds before and behind, and they pretend much truth to the king's grace and to the commonwealth, when they intend nothing less; and deceive the poor ignorant people, and bring them to fight against both the king, the church, and the commonwealth.

They arm them with the sign of the cross and of the wounds, and go clean contrary to him that bare the cross, and suffered those wounds. They rise with the king, and fight against the king in his ministers and officers; they rise with the church, and fight against the church, which is the congregation of faithful men; they rise for the commonwealth, and fight against it, and go about to make the commons each to kill other, and to destroy the commonwealth. Lo, what false pretence can the devil send amongst us? It is one of his most crafty and subtle assaults, to send his warriors forth under the badge of God, as though they were armed in righteousness and justice.

But if we will resist strongly indeed, we must

be clothed or armed with the habergeon of very justice or righteousness; in true obedience to our prince, and faithful love to our neighbours; and take no false quarrels in hand, nor any feigned armour; but in justice, "having your feet shod for [the] preparation of the gospel of peace."

Lo, what manner of battle this warrior St. Paul teacheth us, "to be shod on our feet," that we may go readily and prepare way for the gospel; yea, the gospel of peace, not of rebellion, not of insurrection: no, it teacheth obedience, humility, and quietness; it maketh peace in the conscience, and teacheth true faith in Jesus Christ, and to walk in God's laws armed with God's armour, as Paul teacheth here. Yea, if bishops in England had been "shod for the preparation of this gospel," and had endeavoured themselves to teach and set [it] forth, as our most noble prince hath devised; and if certain gentlemen, being justices, had executed his grace's commandment, in setting forth this gospel of peace, this disturbance among the people had not happened.

But ye say, it is new learning. Now I tell you it is the old learning. Yea, ye say, it is old heresy new scoured. Nay, I tell you it is old truth, long rusted with your canker, and now new made bright and scoured. What a rusty truth is this, *Quodcumque ligaveris,* " Whatsoever thou bindest," &c. This is a truth spoken to the apostles, and all true preachers their successors, that with the law of God they should bind and condemn all that sinned; and whosoever did repent, they should declare him loosed and forgiven, by believing in the blood of Christ. But how hath this truth over-rusted with the pope's rust? For he, by this text, " Whatsoever thou bindeth," hath taken upon him to make what laws him listed, clean contrary unto God's word, which willeth that every man should obey the prince's law: and by this text, " Whatsoever thou loosest," he hath made all people believe that, for money, he might forgive what and whom he lusted; so that if any man had robbed his master, or taken anything wrongfully, the pope would loose him, by this pardon or that pardon, given to these friars or those friars, put in this box or that box. And, as it were, by these means a dividend of the spoil was made, so that it was not restored, nor the person rightly discharged; and yet most part of the spoil came to the hands of him and his ministers. What is this but a new learning; a new canker to rust and corrupt the old truth? Ye call your learning old: it may indeed be called old, for it cometh of that serpent which did pervert God's commandment and beguiled Eve; so it is an old custom to pervert God's word, and to rust it, and corrupt it.

We be a great many that profess to be true ministers of the gospel; but at the trial I think it will come to pass as it did with Gideon, a duke, which God raised up to deliver the children of Israel from the Midianites, in whose hands they were fallen, because they had broken God's commandment, and displeased God: yet at the length he had compassion on them, and raised up Gideon to deliver them. When they heard that they had a captain, or a duke, that should deliver them, they assembled a great number, about thirty thousand:

but when it came to pass that they should fight, they departed all save five hundred. So, I fear me, that at the trial we shall be found but a few ministers of the true gospel of peace, and armed in the true armour of God.

It followeth, " And in all things take the shield or buckler of faith." The buckler is a thing wherewith a man most chiefly defendeth himself: and that must be perfect faith in Jesus Christ, in our Captain, and in his word. It must also be a true faith, it is else no part of the armour of God : it may not be feigned, but a buckler, which may stop or quench the violence of the flaming darts of the most wicked.

"Take also the helmet or head-piece of health," or true health in Jesus Christ; for there is no health in any other name : not the health of a grey friar's coat, or the health of this pardon or that pardon; that were a false helmet, and should not defend the violence of the wicked.

"And the sword of the Spirit, which is the word of God." Lo, St. Paul teacheth you battle; to take in your left hand the shield of faith, to defend and bear off the darts of the devil, and in the other hand a sword to strike with against the enemy: for a good man of war may not stand against, and defend only, but also strike against his enemy. So St. Paul giveth us here a sword, "The word of God." For this sword is it that beateth this great captain, our enemy. Christ himself gave us ensample to fight with this sword; for he answered the devil with the scripture, and said, "It is written." With this sword he drave away the devil: and so let us break his head with this sword, the true word of God, and not with any word of the bishop of Rome's making; not with his old learning, nor his new learning, but with the pure word of God.

The time passeth: I will therefore make an end. Let us fight manfully, and not cease; for no man is crowned or rewarded but in the end. We must therefore fight continually, and with this sword; and thus armed, and we shall receive the reward of victory. And thus the grace of our Lord Jesus Christ be with all your spirits. Amen.

THE SERMON THAT THE REVEREND FATHER IN CHRIST, M. HUGH LATIMER, BISHOP OF WORCESTER, MADE TO THE CONVOCATION OF THE CLERGY, BEFORE THE PARLIAMENT BEGAN, THE 9 DAY OF JUNE, THE 28 YEAR OF THE REIGN OF OUR LATE KING HENRY THE 8. TRANSLATED OUT OF LATIN INTO ENGLISH, TO THE INTENT THAT THINGS WELL SAID TO A FEW MAY BE UNDERSTOOD OF MANY, AND DO GOOD TO ALL THEM THAT DESIRE TO UNDERSTAND THE TRUTH.

Filii hujus seculi, &c.—Luc. xvi.

BRETHREN, ye be come together this day, as far as I perceive, to hear of great and weighty matters. Ye be come together to entreat of things that most appertain to the commonwealth. This being thus, ye look, I am assured, to hear of me, which am commanded to make as a preface this exhortation, (albeit I am unlearned and far unworthy,) such things as shall be much meet for this your assembly. I therefore, not only very desirous to obey the commandment of our Primate, but also right greatly coveting to serve and satisfy all your expectation; lo, briefly, and as plainly as I can, will speak of matters both worthy to be heard in your congregation, and also of such as best shall become mine office in this place. That I may do this the more commodiously, I have taken that notable sentence in which our Lord was not afraid to pronounce "the children of this world to be much more prudent and politic than the children of light in their generation." Neither will I be afraid, trusting that he will aid and guide me to use this sentence, as a good ground and foundation of all such things, as hereafter I shall speak of.

Now, I suppose that you see right well, being men of such learning, for what purpose the Lord said this, and that ye have no need to be holpen with any part of my labour in this thing. But yet, if ye will pardon me, I will wade somewhat deeper in this matter, and as nigh as I can, fetch it from the first original beginning. For undoubtedly, ye may much marvel at this saying, if ye well ponder both what is said, and who saith it. Define me first these three things: what prudence is; what the world; what light; and who be the children of the world; who of the light: see what they signify in scripture. I marvel if by and by ye all agree, that the children of the world should be wiser than the children of the light. To come somewhat nigher the matter, thus the Lord beginneth:

There was a certain rich man that had a steward, which was accused unto him that he had dissipated and wasted his goods. This rich man called his steward to him and said, What is this that I hear of thee? Come, make me an account of thy stewardship; thou mayest no longer bear this office.

BRETHREN, because these words are so spoken in a parable, and are so wrapped in wrinkles, that yet they seem to have a face and a similitude of a thing done indeed, and like an history, I think it much profitable to tarry somewhat in them. And though we may perchance find in our hearts to believe all that is there spoken to be true; yet I doubt whether we may abide it, that these words of Christ do pertain unto us, and admonish us of our duty, which do and live after such sort, as though Christ, when he spake any thing, had, as the time served him, served his turn, and not regarded the time that came after him, neither provided for us, or any matters of ours; as some of the philosophers thought, which said, that God walked up and down in heaven, and thinketh never a deal of our affairs. But, my good brethren, err not you so; stick not you to such your imaginations. For if ye inwardly behold these words, if ye diligently roll them in your minds, and after explicate and open them, ye shall see our time much touched in these mysteries. Ye shall perceive that God by this example shaketh us by the noses and pulleth us by the ears. Ye shall perceive very plain, that God setteth before our eyes in this similitude what we ought most to flee, and what we ought soonest to follow. For Luke saith, "The Lord spake these words to his disciples." Wherefore let it be out of all doubt that he spake them to us, which even as we will be counted the successors and vicars of Christ's disciples, so we be, if we be good dispensers and do our duty. He said these things partly to us, which spake them partly of himself. For he is that rich man, which not only had, but hath, and shall have evermore, I say not one, but many stewards, even to the end of the world.

He is man, seeing that he is God and man. He is rich, not only in mercy but in all kind of riches; for it is he that giveth to us all things abundantly. It is he of whose hand we received both our lives, and other things necessary for the conservation of the same. What man hath any thing, I pray you, but he hath received it of his plentifulness? To be short, it is he that "openeth his hand, and filleth all beasts with his blessing," and giveth unto us in most ample wise his benediction. Neither his treasure can be spent, how much soever he lash out; how much soever we take of him, his treasure tarrieth still, ever taken, never spent.

He is also the good man of the house: the church is his household which ought with all diligence to be fed with his word and his sacraments. These be his goods most precious, the dispensation and administration whereof he would bishops and curates should have. Which thing St. Paul affirmeth, saying, "Let men esteem us as the ministers of Christ, and dispensers of God's mysteries." But, I pray you, what is to be looked for in a dispenser? This surely, "That he be found faithful," and that he truly dispense, and lay out the goods of the Lord; that he give meat in time; give it, I say, and not sell it; meat, I say, and not poison. For the one doth intoxicate and slay the eater, the other feedeth and nourisheth him. Finally, let him not slack and defer the doing of his office, but let him do his duty when time is, and need requireth it. This is also to be looked for, that he be one whom God hath called and put in office, and not one that cometh uncalled, unsent for; not one that of himself presumeth to take honour upon him. And surely, if all this that I say be required in a good minister, it is much lighter to require them all in every one, than to find one any where that hath them all. Who is a true and faithful steward? He is true, he is faithful, that coineth no new money, but taketh it ready coined of the good man of the house; and neither changeth it, nor clippeth it, after it is taken to him to spend, but spendeth even the self-same that he had of his Lord, and spendeth it as his Lord's commandment is; neither to his own vantage uttering it, nor as the lewd servant did, hiding it in the ground. Brethren, if a faithful steward ought to do as I have said, I pray you, ponder and examine this well, whether our bishops and abbots, prelates and curates, have been hitherto faithful stewards or no? Ponder, whether yet many of them be as they should be or no? Go ye to, tell me now as your conscience leadeth you (I will let pass to speak of many other), was there not some, that despising the money of the Lord, as copper and not current, either coined new themselves, or else uttered abroad newly coined of other; sometime either adulterating the word of God or else mingling it (as taverners do, which brew and utter the evil and good both in one pot), sometime in the stead of God's word blowing out the dreams of men? while they thus preached to the people the redemption that cometh by Christ's death to serve only them that died before his coming, that were in the time of the old testament; and that now since redemption and forgiveness of sins purchased by money, and devised by men is of efficacy, and not redemption purchased by Christ (they have a wonderful pretty example to persuade this thing, of a certain married woman, which, when her husband was in purgatory, in that fiery furnace that hath burned away so many of our pence, paid her husband's ransom, and so of duty claimed him to be set at liberty): while they thus preached to the people, that dead images (which at the first, as I think, were set up, only to represent things absent) not only ought to be covered with gold, but also ought of all faithful and christian people (yea, in this scarceness and penury of all things), to be clad with silk garments, and those also laden with precious gems and jewels; and that beside all this, they are to be lighted with wax candles, both within the church and without the church, yea, and at noon days; as who should say, here no cost can be too great; whereas in the mean time we see Christ's faithful and lively images, bought with no less price than with his most precious blood (alas, alas!) to be an hungred, a-thirst, a-cold, and to lie in darkness, wrapped in all wretchedness, yea, to lie there till death take away their miseries: while they preached these will-works, that come but of our own devotion, although they be not so necessary as the works of mercy, and the precepts of God, yet they said, and in the pulpit, that will-works were more principal, more excellent, and (plainly to utter what they mean) more acceptable to God than works of mercy; as though now man's inventions and fancies could please God better than God's precepts, or strange things better than his own: while they thus preached that more fruit, more devotion cometh of the beholding of an image, though it be but a Pater-noster while, than is gotten by reading and contemplation in scripture, though ye read and contemplate therein seven years' space: finally, while they preached thus, souls tormented in purgatory to have most need of our help, and that they can have no aid, but of us in this world: of the which two, if the one be not false, yet at the least it is ambiguous, uncertain, doubtful, and therefore rashly and arrogantly with such boldness affirmed in the audience of the people; the other, by all men's opinions, is manifestly false: I let pass to speak of much other such like counterfeit doctrine, which hath been blasted and blown out by some for the space of three hours together. Be these the Christian and divine mysteries, and not rather the dreams of men? Be these the faithful dispensers of God's mysteries, and not rather false dissipators of them? whom God never put in office, but rather the devil set them over a miserable family, over an house miserably ordered and entreated. Happy were the people if such preached seldom.

And yet it is a wonder to see these, in their

generation, to be much more prudent and politic than the faithful ministers are in their generation; while they go about more prudently to stablish men's dreams, than these do to hold up God's commandments.

Thus it cometh to pass that works lucrative, will-works, men's fancies reign; but christian works, necessary works, fruitful works, be trodden under the foot. Thus the evil is much better set out by evil men, than the good by good men; because the evil be more wise than be the good in their generation. These be the false stewards, whom all good and faithful men every day accuse unto the rich master of the household, not without great heaviness, that they waste his goods; whom he also one day will call to him, and say to them as he did to his steward, when he said, "What is this that I hear of thee?" Here God partly wondereth at our ingratitude and perfidy, partly chideth us for them; and being both full of wonder and ready to chide, asketh us, "What is this that I hear of you?" As though he should say unto us; " All good men in all places complain of you, accuse your avarice, your exactions, your tyranny. They have required in you a long season, and yet require, diligence and sincerity. I commanded you, that with all industry and labour ye should feed my sheep : ye earnestly feed yourselves from day to day, wallowing in delights and idleness. I commanded you to teach my commandments, and not your fancies; and that ye should seek my glory and my vantage : you teach your own traditions, and seek your own glory and profit. You preach very seldom ; and when ye do preach, do nothing but cumber them that preach truly, as much as lieth in you : that it were much better such were not to preach at all, than so perniciously to preach. Oh, what hear I of you? You, that ought to be my preachers, what other thing do you, than apply all your study hither, to bring all my preachers to envy, shame, contempt? Yea, more than this, ye pull them into perils, into prisons, and, as much as in you lieth, to cruel deaths. To be short, I would that christian people should hear my doctrine, and at their convenient leisure read it also, as many as would: your care is not that all men may hear it, but all your care is, that no lay man do read it: surely, being afraid lest they by the reading should understand it, and understanding, learn to rebuke our slothfulness. This is your generation, this is your dispensation, this is your wisdom. In this generation, in this dispensation, you be most politic, most witty. These be the things that I hear of your demeanour. I wished to hear better report of you. Have ye thus deceived me? or have ye rather deceived yourselves? Where I had but one house, that is to say, the church, and this so dearly beloved of me, that for the love of her I put myself forth to be slain, and to shed my blood; this church at my departure I committed unto your charge, to be fed, to be nourished, and to be made much of. My pleasure was ye should occupy my place; my desire was ye should have borne like love to this church, like fatherly affection, as I did: I made you my vicars, yea, in matters of most importance.

"For thus I taught openly: 'He that should hear you, should hear me; he that should despise you, should despise me.' I gave you also keys, not earthly keys, but heavenly. I left my goods that I have evermore most highly esteemed, that is, my word and sacraments, to be dispensed of you. These benefits I gave you, and do you give me these thanks? Can you find in your hearts thus to abuse my goodness, my benignity, my gentleness? Have you thus deceived me? No, no, ye have not deceived me, but yourselves. My gifts and benefits towards you shall be to your greater damnation. Because you have contemned the lenity and clemency of the master of the house, ye have right well deserved to abide the rigour and severity of the judge. Come forth then, let us see an account of your stewardship. An horrible and fearful sentence: Ye may have no longer my goods in your hands. A voice to weep at, and to make men tremble!"

You see, brethren, you see, what evil the evil stewards must come to. Your labour is paid for, if ye can so take heed, that no such sentence be spoken to you; nay, we must all take heed lest these threatenings one day take place in us. But lest the length of my sermon offend you too sore, I will leave the rest of the parable and take me to the handling of the end of it; that is, I will declare unto you how the children of this world be more witty, crafty, and subtle, than are the children of the light in their generation. Which sentence would God it lay in my poor tongue to explicate with such light of words, that I might seem rather to have painted it before your eyes, than to have spoken it; and that you might rather seem to see the thing, than to hear it! But I confess plainly this thing to be far above my power. Therefore this being only left to me, I wish for that I have not, and am sorry that that is not in me which I would so gladly have, that is, power so to handle the thing that I have in hand, that all that I say may turn to the glory of God, your souls' health, and the edifying of Christ's body Wherefore I pray you all to pray with me unto God, and that in your petition you desire, that these two things he vouchsafe to grant us, first, a mouth for me to speak rightly; next, ears for you, that in hearing me ye may take profit at my hand: and that this may come to effect, you shall desire him, unto whom our master Christ bad we should pray, saying even the same prayer that he himself did institute. Wherein ye shall pray for our most gracious sovereign lord the king, chief and supreme head of the church of England under Christ, and for the most excellent, gracious, and virtuous lady queen Jane, his most lawful wife, and for all his, whether they be of the clergy or laity, whether they be of the nobility, or else other his grace's subjects, not forgetting those that being departed out of this transitory life, and now sleep in the sleep of peace, and rest from their labours in quietness and peaceable sleep, faithfully, lovingly, and patiently looking for that that they clearly shall see when God shall be so pleased. For all these, and for grace necessary, ye shall say unto God God's prayer, *Pater-noster.*

THE SECOND SERMON, IN THE AFTERNOON.

Filii hujus seculi, &c.—Luc. xvi. [8].

CHRIST in this saying touched the sloth and sluggishness of his, and did not allow the fraud and subtlety of others; neither was glad that it was indeed as he had said, but complained rather that it should be so: as many men speak many things, not that they ought to be so, but that they are wont to be so. Nay, this grieved Christ, that the children of this world should be of more policy than the children of light; which thing was true in Christ's time, and now in our time is most true. Who is so blind but he seeth this clearly; except perchance there be any that cannot discern the children of the world from the children of light? The children of the world conceive and bring forth more prudently; and things conceived and brought forth they nourish and conserve with much more policy than do the children of light. Which thing is as sorrowful to be said, as it seemeth absurd to be heard. When ye hear the children of the world, you understand the world as a father. For the world is father of many children, not by the first creation and work, but by imitation of love. He is not only a father, but also the son of another father. If ye know once his father, by and by ye shall know his children. For he that hath the devil to his father, must needs have devilish children. The devil is not only taken for father, but also for prince of the world, that is, of worldly folk. It is either all one thing, or else not much different, to say, children of the world, and children of the devil; according to that that Christ said to the Jews, "Ye are of your father the devil:" where as undoubtedly he spake to children of this world. Now seeing the devil is both author and ruler of the darkness, in the which the children of this world walk, or, to say better, wander; they mortally hate both the light, and also the children of light. And hereof it cometh, that the children of light never, or very seldom, lack persecution in this world, unto which the children of the world, that is, of the devil, bringeth them. And there is no man but he seeth, that these use much more policy in procuring the hurt and damage of the good, than those in defending themselves. Therefore, brethren, gather you the disposition and study of the children by the disposition and study of the fathers. Ye know this is a proverb much used: "An evil crow, an evil egg." Then the children of this world that are known to have so evil a father, the world, so evil a grandfather, the devil, cannot choose but be evil. Surely the first head of their ancestry was the deceitful serpent the devil, a monster monstrous above all monsters. I cannot wholly express him, I wot not what to call him, but a certain thing altogether made of the hatred of God, of mistrust in God, of lyings, deceits, perjuries, discords, manslaughters; and, to say at one word, a thing concrete, heaped up and made of all kind of mischief. But what the devil mean I to go about to describe particularly the devil's nature, when no reason, no power of man's mind can comprehend it? This alonely I can say grossly, and as in a sum, of the which all we (our hurt is the more) have experience, the devil to be a stinking sentine of all vices; a foul filthy channel of all mischiefs; and that this world, his son, even a child meet to have such a parent, is not much unlike his father.

Then, this devil being such one as can never be unlike himself; lo, of Envy, his well-beloved Leman, he begat the World, and after left it with Discord at nurse; which World, after that it came to man's state, had of many concubines many sons. He was so fecund a father, and had gotten so many children of Lady Pride, Dame Gluttony, Mistress Avarice, Lady Lechery, and of Dame Subtlety, that now hard and scant ye may find any corner, any kind of life, where many of his children be not. In court, in cowls, in cloisters, in rochets, be they never so white; yea, where shall ye not find them? Howbeit, they that be secular and laymen, are not by and by children of the world; nor they children of light, that are called spiritual, and of the clergy. No, no; as ye may find among the laity many children of light, so among the clergy, (how much soever we arrogate these holy titles unto us, and think them only attributed to us, *Vos estis lux mundi, peculium Christi, &c.* "Ye are the light of the world, the chosen people of Christ, a kingly priesthood, an holy nation, and such other,") ye shall find many children of the world; because in all places the world getteth many children. Among the lay people the world ceaseth not to bring to pass, that as they be called wordly, so they are wordly indeed; driven headlong by worldly desires: insomuch that they may right well seem to have taken as well the manners as the name of their father. In the clergy, the world also hath learned a way to make of men spiritual, worldlings; yea, and there also to form worldly children, where with great pretence of holiness, and crafty colour of religion, they utterly desire to hide and cloak the name of the world, as though they were ashamed of their father; which do execrate and detest the world (being nevertheless their father) in words and outward signs, but in heart and work they coll and kiss him, and in all their lives declare themselves to be his babes; insomuch that in all worldly points they far pass and surmount those that they call seculars, laymen, men of the world. The child so diligently followeth the steps of his father, is never destitute of the aid of his grandfather. These be our holy holy men, that say they are dead to the world, when no men be more lively in worldly things than some of them be. But let them be in profession and name most farthest from the world, most alienate from it; yea, so far, that they may seem to have no occupying, no kindred, no affinity, nothing to do with it: yet in their life and deeds they shew themselves no bastards, but right begotten children of the world; as that which the world long sithens had by his dear wife Dame Hypocrisy, and since hath brought them up and multiplied to more than a good many; increased them too much, albeit they swear by all he-saints and she-saints too, that they know not their father, nor mother, neither the world, nor hypocrisy; as indeed they can semble and dissemble all things; which thing they might learn wonderful well of their parents. I speak not of all religious men, but of those that the world hath fast knit at his girdle, even in the midst of their religion, that is, of many and more than many. For I fear, lest in all orders of men the better, I must say the greater part of them be out of order, and children of the world. Many of these might seem ingrate and unkind children, that will no better acknowledge and recognise their parents in words and outward pretence, but abrenounce and cast them off, as though they hated them as dogs and serpents. Howbeit they, in this wise, are most grateful to their parents, because they be most like them, so lively representing them in countenance and conditions, that their parents seem in them to be young again, forasmuch as they ever say one thing and think another. They shew themselves to be as sober, as temperate, as Curius the Roman was, and live every day as though all their life were a shroving time. They be like their parents,

I say, inasmuch as they, in following them, seem and make men believe they hate them. Thus grandfather Devil, father World, and mother Hypocrisy, have brought them up. Thus good obedient sons have borne away their parents' commandments; neither these be solitary, how religious, how mocking, how monking, I would say, soever they be.

O ye will lay this to my charge, that *monachus* and *solitarius* signifieth all one. I grant this to be so, yet these be so solitary that they be not alone, but accompanied with great flocks of fraternities. And I marvel if there be not a great sort of bishops and prelates, that are brethren germain unto these; and as a great sort, so even as right born, and world's children by as good title as they. But because I cannot speak of all, when I say prelates, I understand bishops, abbots, priors, archdeacons, deans, and other of such sort, that are now called to this convocation, as I see, to entreat here of nothing but of such matters as both appertain to the glory of Christ, and to the wealth of the people of England. Which thing I pray God they do as earnestly as they ought to do. But it is to be feared lest, as light hath many her children here, so the world hath sent some of his whelps hither; amongst the which I know there can be no concord nor unity, albeit they be in one place, in one congregation. I know there can be no agreement between these two, as long as they have minds so unlike, and so contrary affections, judgments so utterly diverse in all points. But if the children of this world be either more in number, or more prudent than the children of light, what then availeth us to have this convocation? Had it not been better we had not been called together at all? For as the children of this world be evil, so they breed and bring forth things evil; and yet there be more of them in all places, or at the least they be more politic than the children of light in their generation. And here I speak of the generation whereby they do engender, and not of that whereby they are engendered, because it should be too long to entreat how the children of light are engendered, and how they come in at the door; and how the children of the world be engendered, and come in another way. Howbeit, I think all you that be here were not engendered after one generation, neither that ye all came by your promotions after one manner: God grant that ye, engendered worldly, do not engender worldly: and as now I much pass not how ye were engendered, or by what means ye were promoted to those dignities that ye now occupy, so it be honest, good and profitable, that ye in this your consultation shall do and engender.

The end of your convocation shall shew what ye have done; the fruit that shall come of your consultation shall shew what generation ye be of. For what have ye done hitherto, I pray you, these seven years and more? What have ye engendered? What have ye brought forth? What fruit is come of your long and great assembly? What one thing that the people of England hath been the better of a hair; or you yourselves, either more accepted before God, or better discharged toward the people committed unto your cure? For that the people is better learned and taught now, than they were in time past, to whether of these ought we to attribute it, to your industry, or to the providence of God, and the foreseeing of the king's grace! Ought we to thank you, or the king's highness? Whether stirred other first, you the king, that he might preach, or he you by his letters, that ye should preach oftener? Is it unknown, think you, how both ye and your curates were, in [a] manner, by violence enforced to let books to be made, not by you, but by profane and lay persons; to let them, I say, be sold abroad, and read for the instruction of the people? I am bold with you, but I speak Latin and not English, to the clergy, not to the laity; I speak to you being present, and not behind your backs. God is my witness, I speak whatsoever is spoken of the good-will that I bear you; God is my witness, which knoweth my heart, and compelleth me to say that I say.

Now, I pray you in God's name, what did you, so great fathers, so many, so long a season, so oft assembled together? What went you about? What would ye have brought to pass? Two things taken away—the one, that ye (which I heard) burned a dead man; the other, that ye (which I felt) went about to burn one being alive: him, because he did, I cannot tell how, in his testament withstand your profit; in other points, as I have heard, a very good man; reported to be of an honest life while he lived, full of good works, good both to the clergy, and also to the laity: this other, which truly never hurt any of you, ye would have raked in the coals, because he would not subscribe to certain articles that took away the supremacy of the king:—take away these two noble acts, and there is nothing else left that ye went about, that I know, saving that I now remember, that somewhat ye attempted against Erasmus, albeit as yet nothing is come to light. Ye have oft sat in consultation, but what have ye done? Ye have had many things in deliberation, but what one is put forth, whereby either Christ is more glorified, or else Christ's people made more holy? I appeal to your own conscience. How chanced this? How came it thus? Because there were no children of light, no children of God amongst you, which, setting the world at nought, would study to illustrate the glory of God, and thereby shew themselves children of light? I think not so, certainly I think not so. God forbid, that all you, which were gathered together under the pretence of light, should be children of the world! Then why happened this? Why, I pray you? Perchance, either because the children of the world were more in number in this your congregation, as it oft happeneth, or at the least of more policy than the children of light in their generation: whereby it might very soon be brought to pass, that these were much more stronger in gendering the evil than these in producing the good. The children of light have policy, but it is like the policy of the serpent, and is joined with doveish simplicity. They engender nothing but simply, faithfully, and plainly, even so doing all that they do. And therefore they may with more facility be cumbered in their engendering, and be the more ready to take injuries. But the children of this world have worldly policy, foxly craft, lion-like cruelty, power to do hurt, more than either *aspis* or *basiliscus*, engendering and doing all things fraudulently, deceitfully, guilefully: which as Nimrods and such sturdy and stout hunters, being full of simulation and dissimulation before the Lord, deceive the children of light, and cumber them easily. Hunters go not forth in every man's sight, but do their affairs closely, and with use of guile and deceit wax every day more craftier than other.

The children of this world be like crafty hunters; they be misnamed children of light, forasmuch as they so hate light, and so study to do the works of darkness. If they were the children of light, they would not love darkness. It is no marvel that they go about to keep other in darkness, seeing they be in darkness, from top to toe overwhelmed with darkness, darker than is the darkness of hell. Wherefore it is well done in all orders of men, but especial in the order of prelates, to put a difference between children of light and children of the world, because great deceit ariseth in taking the one for the other. Great imposture cometh, when they that the common people take for the light, go about to take the sun and the light out of the world. But these be easily known, both by the diversity of minds, and also their armours. For whereas the children of light are thus minded, that they seek their adversaries' health, wealth, and profit, with loss of their own commodities, and ofttimes with jeopardy of their life; the children of the world, contrariwise, have such stomachs, that they will sooner see them dead that doth them good, than sustain any loss of temporal things. The armour of the children of light are, first, the word of God, which they ever set forth, and with all diligence put it abroad, that, as much as in them lieth, it may bring forth fruit: after this, patience and prayer, with the which in all adversities the Lord comforteth them. Other things they commit to

God, unto whom they leave all revengement. The armour of the children of the world are, sometime frauds and deceits, sometime lies and money: by the first they make their dreams, their traditions; by the second they stablish and confirm their dreams, be they never so absurd, never so against scripture, honesty, or reason. And if any man resist them, even with these weapons they procure to slay him. Thus they bought Christ's death, the very light itself, and obscured him after his death: thus they buy every day the children of light, and obscure them, and shall so do, until the world be at an end. So that it may be ever true, that Christ said: "The children of the world be wiser, &c."

These worldlings pull down the lively faith, and full confidence that men have in Christ, and set up another faith, another confidence, of their own making: the children of light contrary. These worldlings set little by such works as God hath prepared for our salvation, but they extol traditions and works of their own invention: the children of light contrary. The worldlings, if they spy profit,

D—8

gains, or lucre in any thing, be it never such a trifle, be it never so pernicious, they preach it to the people (if they preach at any time), and these things they defend with tooth and nail. They can scarce disallow the abuses of these, albeit they be intolerable, lest in disallowing the abuse they lose part of their profit. The children of the light contrary, put all things in their degree, best highest, next next, the worst lowest. They extol things necessary, Christian, and commanded of God. They pull down will-works feigned by men, and put them in their place. The abuses of all things they earnestly rebuke. But yet these things be so done on both parties, and so they both do gender, that the children of the world shew themselves wiser than the children of light, and that frauds and deceits, lies and money, seem evermore to have the upper hand. I hold my peace; I will not say how fat feasts, and jolly banquets, be jolly instruments to set forth worldly matters withal. Neither the children of the world be only wiser than the children of light, but are also some of them among themselves much wiser than the other in their generation. For albeit, as touching the end, the generation of them all is one; yet in this same generation some of them have more craftily engendered than the other of their fellows.

For what a thing was that, that once every hundred year was brought forth in Rome of the children of this world, and with how much policy it was made, ye heard at Paul's Cross in the beginning of the last parliament: how some brought forth canonizations, some expectations, some pluralities and unions, some tot-quots and dispensations, some pardons, and these of wonderful variety, some stationaries, some jubilaries, some pocularies for drinkers, some manuaries for handlers of relicks, some pedaries for pilgrims, some oscularies for kissers; some of them engendered one, some other such fetures, and every one in that he was delivered of, was excellent politic, wise; yea, so wise, that with their wisdom they had almost made all the world fools.

But yet they that begot and brought forth that

our old ancient purgatory pick-purse; that that was swaged and cooled with a Franciscan's cowl, put upon a dead man's back, to the fourth part of his sins; that that was utterly to be spoiled, and of none other but of our most prudent lord Pope, and of him as oft as him listed; that satisfactory, that missal, that scalary: they, I say, that were the wise fathers and genitors of this purgatory, were in my mind the wisest of all their generation, and so far pass the children of light, and also the rest of their company, that they both are but fools, if ye compare them with these. It was a pleasant fiction, and from the beginning so profitable to the feigners of it, that almost, I dare boldly say, there hath been no emperor that hath gotten more by taxes and tallages of them that were alive, than these, the very and right-begotten sons of the world, got by dead men's tributes and gifts. If there be some in England, that would this sweeting of the world to be with no less policy kept still than it was born and brought forth in Rome, who then can accuse Christ of lying? No, no; as it hath been ever true, so it shall be, that the children of the world be much wiser, not only in making their things, but also in conserving them. I wot not what it is, but somewhat it is I wot, that some men be so loth to see the abuse of this monster, purgatory, which abuse is more than abominable: as who should say, there is none abuse in it, or else as though there can be none in it. They may seem heartily to love the old thing, that thus earnestly endeavour them to restore him his old name. They would not set an hair by the name, but for the thing. They be not so ignorant (no, they be crafty), but that they know if the name come again, the thing will come after. Thereby it ariseth, that some men make their cracks, that they, maugre all men's heads, have found · purgatory. I cannot tell what is found. This, to pray for dead folks, this is not found, for it was never lost. How can that be found that was not lost? O subtle finders, that can find things, if God will, ere they be lost! For that cowlish deliverance, their scalary losings, their papal spoliations, and other such their figments, they cannot find. No, these be so lost, as they themselves grant, that though they seek them never so diligently, yet they shall not find them, except perchance they hope to see them come in again with their names; and that then money-gathering may return again, and deceit walk about the country, and so stablish their kingdom in all kingdoms. But to what end this chiding between the children of the world and the children of light will come, only he knoweth that once shall judge them both.

Now, to make haste and to come somewhat nigher the end. Go ye to, good brethren and fathers, for the love of God, go ye to; and seeing we are here assembled, let us do something whereby we may be known to be the children of light. Let us do somewhat, lest we, which hitherto have been judged children of the world, seem even still to be so. All men call us prelates: then, seeing we be in council, let us so order ourselves, that we be prelates in honour and dignity; so we may be prelates in holiness, benevolence, diligence, and sincerity. All men know that we be here gathered, and with most fervent desire they anheale, breathe, and gape for the fruit of our convocation : as our acts shall be, so they shall name us : so that now it lieth in us, whether we will be called children of the world, or children of light.

Wherefore lift up your heads, brethren, and look about with your eyes, spy what things are to be reformed in the church of England. Is it so hard, is it so great a matter for you to see many abuses in the clergy, many in the laity? What is done in the Arches? Nothing to be amended? What do they there? Do they evermore rid the people's business and matters, or cumber and ruffle them? Do they evermore correct vice, or else defend it, sometime being well corrected in other places? How many sentences be given there in time, as they ought to be? If men say truth, how many without bribes? Or if all things be well done there, what do men in bishops' Consistories? Shall you often see the punishments assigned by the laws, executed, or else money-redemptions used in their stead? How think you by the ceremonies that are in England, oft-times, with no little offence of weak consciences, contemned; more oftener with superstition so defiled, and so depraved, that you may doubt whether it were better some of them to tarry still, or utterly to take them away? Have not our forefathers complained of the ceremonies, of the superstition, and estimation of them?

Do ye see nothing in our holidays? of the which very few were made at the first, and they to set forth goodness, virtue, and honesty: but sithens, in some places, there is neither mean nor measure in making new holidays, as who should say, this one thing is serving of God, to make this law, that no man may work. But what doth the people on these holidays? Do they give themselves to godliness, or else ungodliness? See ye nothing, brethren? If you see not, yet God seeth. God seeth all the whole holidays to be spent miserably in drunkenness, in glossing, in strife, in envy, in dancing, dicing, idleness, and gluttony. He seeth all this, and threateneth punishment for it. He seeth it, which neither is deceived in seeing, nor deceiveth when he threatneth.

Thus men serve the devil; for God is not thus served, albeit ye say ye serve God. No, the devil hath more service done unto him on one holiday, than on many working days. Let all these abuses be counted as nothing, who is he that is not sorry, to see in so many holidays rich and wealthy persons to flow in delicates, and men that live by their travail, poor men, to lack necessary meat and drink for their wives and their children, and that they cannot labour upon the holidays, except they will be cited, and brought before our Officials? Were it not the office of good prelates to consult upon these matters, and to seek some remedy for them? Ye shall see, my brethren, ye shall see once, what will come of this our winking.

What think ye of these images that are had more than their fellows in reputation; that are gone unto with such labour and weariness of the body, frequented with such our cost, sought out and visited with such confidence? What say ye by these images, that are so famous, so noble, so noted, being of them so many and so divers in England? Do you think that this preferring of picture to picture, image to image, is the right use, and not rather the abuse, of images? But you will say to me, Why make ye all these interrogations? and why, in these your demands, do you let and withdraw the good devotion of the people? Be not all things well done, that are done with good intent, when they be profitable to us? So, surely, covetousness both thinketh and speaketh. Were it not better for us, more for estimation, more meeter for men in our places, to cut away a piece of this our profit, if we will not cut away all, than to wink at such ungodliness, and so long to wink for a little lucre; specially if it be ungodliness, and also seem unto you ungodliness? These be two things, so oft to seek mere images, and sometime to visit the relicks of saints. And yet, as in those there may be much ungodliness committed, so there may here some superstition be hid, if that sometime we chance to visit pigs' bones instead of saints' relicks, as in time past it hath chanced, I had almost said, in England. Then this is too great a blindness, a darkness too sensible, that these should be so commended in sermons of some men, and preached to be done after such manner, as though they could not be evil done; which, notwithstanding, are such, that neither God nor man commandeth them to be done. No, rather, men commanded them either not to be done at all, or else more slowlier and seldomer to be done, forasmuch as our ancestors made this constitution: "We command the priests that they oft admonish the people, and in especial women, that they make no vows but after long deliberation, consent of their husbands and counsel of the priest." The church of England in time past made this constitution. What saw they that made this decree? They saw the intolerable abuses of images. They saw the perils that might ensue of going on pilgrimage. They saw the superstitious difference that men made between image and image. Surely, somewhat they saw. The constitution is so made, that in manner it taketh away all such pilgrimages. For it so plucketh away the abuse of them, that it leaveth either none or else seldom use of them. For they that restrain making vows for going of pilgrimage, restrain also pilgrimage; seeing that for the most part it is seen that few go on pilgrimage but vow-makers, and such as by promise bind themselves to go. And when, I pray you, should a man's wife go on pilgrimage, if she went not before she had well debated the matter with herself, and obtained the consent of her husband, being a wise man, and were also counselled by a learned priest so to do? When should she go far off to these famous images? For this the common people of England think to be going on pilgrimage; to go to some dead and notable image out of town, that is to say, far from their house. Now if your forefathers made this constitution, and yet thereby did nothing, the abuses every day more and more increased, what is left for you to do? Brethren and fathers, if ye purpose to do any thing, what should ye sooner do, than to take utterly away these deceitful and juggling images; or else, if ye know any other mean to put away abuses, to shew it, if ye intend to remove abuses? Methink it should be grateful and pleasant to you to mark the earnest mind of your forefathers, and to look upon their desire where they say in their constitution, "We *command* you," and not, "We *counsel* you." How have we been so long a-cold, so long slack in setting forth so wholesome a precept of the church of England, where we be so hot in all things that have any gains in them, albeit they be neither commanded us, nor yet given us by counsel; as though we had lever the abuse of things should tarry still than, it taken away, lose our profit? To let pass the solemn and nocturnal bacchanals, the prescript miracles, that are done upon certain days in the west part of England, who hath not heard? I think ye have heard of St. Blesis's heart which is at Malverne, and of St. Algar's bones, how long they deluded the people: I am afraid, to the loss of many souls. Whereby men may well conjecture, that all about in this realm there is plenty of such juggling deceits. And yet hitherto ye have sought no remedy. But even still the miserable people are suffered to take the false miracles for the true, and to lie still asleep in all kind of superstition. God have mercy upon us!

Last of all, how think you of matrimony? Is all well here? What of baptism? Shall we evermore in ministering of it speak Latin, and not in English rather, that the people may know what is said and done?

What think ye of these mass-priests, and of the masses themselves? What say ye? Be all things here so without abuses, that nothing ought to be amended? Your forefathers saw somewhat, which made this constitution against the venality and sale of masses, that, under pain of suspending, no priest should sell his saying of tricennals or annals What saw they, that made this constitution? What priests saw they? What manner of masses saw they, trow ye? But at the last, what became of so good a constitution? God have mercy upon us! If there be nothing to be amended abroad, concerning the whole, let every one of us make one better: if there be neither abroad nor at home any thing to be amended and redressed, my lords, be ye of good cheer, be merry; and at the least, because we have nothing else to do, let us reason the matter how we may be richer. Let us fall to some pleasant communication; after let us go home, even as good as we came hither, that is, right-begotten children of the world, and utterly worldlings. And while we live here, let us all make bone cheer. For after this life there is small pleasure, little mirth for us to hope for; if now there be nothing to be changed in our fashions. Let us say, not as St. Peter did, "Our end approacheth nigh," this is an heavy hearing; but let us say as the evil servant said, "It will be long ere my master come." This is pleasant. Let us beat our fellows: let us eat and drink with drunkards. Surely, as oft as we do not take away the abuse of things, so oft we beat our fellows. As oft as we give not the people their true food, so oft we beat our fellows. As oft as we let them die in superstition, so oft we beat them. To be short, as oft as we blind lead them blind, so oft we beat, and grievously beat our fellows. When we welter in pleasures and idleness, then we eat and drink with drunkards. But God will come, God will come, he will not tarry long away. He will come upon such a day as we nothing look for him, and at such hour as we know not. He will come and cut us in pieces. He will reward us as he doth the hypocrites. He will set us where wailing shall be, my brethren; where gnashing of teeth shall be, my brethren. And let here be the end of our tragedy, if ye will. These be the delicate dishes prepared for the world's well-beloved children. These be the wafers and junkets provided for worldly prelates—wailing and gnashing of teeth. Can there be any mirth, where these two courses last all the feast? Here we laugh, there we shall weep. Our teeth make merry here, ever dashing in delicates; there we shall be torn with teeth, and do nothing but gnash and grind our own. To what end have we now excelled other in policy? What have we brought forth at the last? Ye see, brethren, what sorrow, what punishment is provided for you, if ye be worldlings. If ye will not thus be vexed, be ye not the children of the world. If ye will not be the children of the world, be not stricken with the love of worldly things; lean not upon them. If ye will not die eternally, live not worldly. Come, go to; leave the love of your profit; study for the glory and profit of Christ; seek in your consultations such things as pertain to Christ, and bring forth at the last somewhat that may please Christ. Feed ye tenderly, with all diligence, the flock of Christ. Preach truly the word of God. Love the light, walk in the light, and so be ye the children of light while ye are in this world, that ye may shine in the world that is to come bright as the sun, with the Father, the Son, and the Holy Ghost; to whom be all honour, praise, and glory. Amen.

A SERMON OF THE REVEREND FATHER MASTER HUGH LATIMER, PREACHED IN THE SHROUDS AT ST. PAUL'S CHURCH IN LONDON, ON THE EIGHTEENTH DAY OF JANUARY, ANNO 1548.

Quæcunque scripta sunt ad nostram doctrinam scripta sunt.—
Rom. xv. 4.

"ALL things which are written, are written for our erudition and knowledge. All things that are written in God's book, in the Bible book, in the book of the holy scripture, are written to be our doctrine."

I told you in my first sermon, honourable audience, that I purposed to declare unto you two things. The one, what seed should be sown in God's field, in God's plough land; and the other, who should be the sowers: that is to say, what doctrine is to be taught in Christ's church and congregation, and what men should be the teachers and preachers of it. The first part I have told you in the three sermons past, in which I have assayed to set forth my plough, to prove what I could do. And now I shall tell you who be the ploughers: for God's word is a seed to be sown in God's field, that is, the faithful congregation, and the preacher is the sower. And it is in the gospel: *Exivit qui seminat seminare semen suum;* "He that soweth, the husbandman, the ploughman, went forth to sow his seed." So that a preacher is resembled to a ploughman, as it is in another place: *Nemo admota aratro manu, et a tergo respiciens, aptus est regno Dei.* "No man that putteth his hand to the plough, and looketh back, is apt for the kingdom of God." That is to say, let no preacher be negligent in doing his office. Albeit this is one of the places that hath been racked, as I told you of racking scriptures. And I have been one of them myself that hath racked it, I cry God mercy for it; and have been one of them that have believed and expounded it against religious persons that would forsake their order which they had professed, and would go out of their cloister: whereas indeed it toucheth not monkery, nor maketh any thing at all for any such matter; but it is directly spoken of diligent preaching of the word of God.

For preaching of the gospel is one of God's plough-works, and the preacher is one of God's ploughmen. Ye may not be offended with my similitude, in that I compare preaching to the labour and work of ploughing, and the preacher to a ploughman: ye may not be offended with this my similitude; for I have been slandered of some persons for such things. It hath been said of me, "Oh, Latimer! nay, as for him, I will never believe him while I live, nor never trust him; for he likened our blessed lady to a saffron-bag:" where indeed I never used that similitude. But it was, as I have said unto you before now, according to that which Peter saw before in the spirit of prophecy, and said, that there should come after men *per quos via veritatis maledictis afficeretur;* there should come fellows "by whom the way of truth should be evil spoken of, and slandered." But in case I had used this similitude, it had not been to be reproved, but might have been without reproach. For I might have said thus: as the saffron-bag that hath been full of saffron, or hath had saffron in it, doth ever after savour and smell of the sweet saffron that it contained; so our blessed lady, which conceived and bare Christ in her womb, did ever after resemble the manners and virtues of that precious babe that she bare. And what had our blessed lady been the worse for this? or what dishonour was this to our blessed lady? But as preachers must be wary and circumspect, that they give not any just occasion to be slandered and ill spoken of by the hearers, so must not the auditors be offended without cause. For heaven is in the gospel likened to a mustard-seed: it is compared also to a piece of leaven; and as Christ saith, that at the last day he will come like a thief: and what dishonour is this to God? or what derogation is this to heaven? Ye may not then, I say, be offended with my similitude, for because I liken preaching to a ploughman's labour, and a prelate to a ploughman. But now you will ask me, whom I call a prelate? A prelate is that man, whatsoever he be, that hath a flock to be taught of him; whosoever hath any spiritual charge in the faithful congregation, and whosoever he be that hath cure of souls. And well may the preacher and the ploughman be likened together: first, for their labour of all seasons of the year; for there is no time of the year in which the ploughman hath not some special work to do: as in my country in Leicestershire, the ploughman hath a time to set forth, and to assay his plough, and other times for other necessary works to be done. And then they also may be likened together for the diversity of works and variety of offices that they have to do. For as the ploughman first setteth forth his plough, and then tilleth his land, and breaketh it in furrows, and sometime ridgeth it up again; and at another time harroweth it and clotteth it, and sometime dungeth it and hedgeth it, diggeth it and weedeth it, purgeth and maketh it clean: so the prelate, the preacher, hath many diverse offices to do. He hath first a busy work to bring his parishioners to a right faith, as Paul calleth it, and not a swerving faith; but to a faith that embraceth Christ, and trusteth to his merits; a lively faith, a justifying faith; a faith that maketh a man righteous, without respect of works: as ye have it very well declared and set forth in the Homily. He hath then a busy work, I say, to bring his flock to a right faith, and then to confirm them in the same faith: now casting them down with the law, and with threatenings of God for sin; now ridging them up again with the gospel, and with the promises of God's favour: now weeding them, by telling them their faults, and making them forsake sin; now clotting them, by breaking their stony hearts, and by making them supplehearted, and making them to have hearts of flesh; that is, soft hearts, and apt for doctrine to enter in: now teaching to know God rightly, and to know their duty to God and their neighbours: now exhorting them, when they know their duty, that they do it, and be diligent in it; so that they have a continual work to do. Great is their business, and therefore great should be their hire. They have great labours, and therefore they ought to have good livings, that they may commodiously feed their flock; for the preaching of the word of God unto the people is called meat: scripture calleth it meat; not strawberries, that come but once a year, and tarry not long, but are soon gone: but it is meat, it is no dainties. The people must have meat that must be familiar and continual, and daily given unto them to feed upon. Many make a strawberry of it, ministering it but once a year; but such do not the office of good prelates. For Christ saith, *Quis putas est servus prudens et fidelis? Qui dat cibum in tempore.* "Who think you is a wise and faithful servant? He that giveth meat in due time." So that he must at all times convenient preach diligently: therefore saith he, "Who trow ye is a faithful servant?" He speaketh it as though it were a rare thing to find such a one, and as though he should say, there be but a few of them to find in the world. And how few of them there be throughout this realm that give meat to their flock as they should do, the Visitors can best tell. Too few, too few; the more is the pity, and never so few as now.

By this, then, it appeareth that a prelate, or any that hath cure of soul, must diligently and substantially work and labour. Therefore saith Paul to Timothy, *Qui episcopatum desiderat, hic bonum opus desiderat:* "He that desireth to have the office of a bishop, or a prelate, that man desireth a good work." Then if it be a good work, it is work; ye can make but a work of it. It is God's work, God's plough, and that plough God would have still going. Such then as loiter and live idly, are not good prelates, or ministers. And of such as do not preach and teach, nor do their duties, God saith by his prophet Jeremy, *Maledictus qui facit opus Dei fraudulenter;* "Cursed be the man that doth the work of God fraudulently, guilefully or deceitfully:" some books have it *negligenter*, "negligently or slackly." How many such prelates, how many such bishops, Lord, for thy mercy, are there now in England! And what shall we in this case do? shall we company with them? O Lord, for thy mercy! shall we not company with them? O Lord, whither shall we flee from them? But "cursed be he that doth the work of God negligently or guilefully." A sore word for them that are negligent in discharging their office, or have done it fraudulently; for that is the thing that maketh the people ill.

But true it must be that Christ saith, *Multi sunt vocati, pauci vero electi:* "Many are called, but few are chosen." Here have I an occasion by the way somewhat to say unto you; yea, for the place I alleged unto you before out of Jeremy, the forty-eighth chapter. And it was spoken of a spiritual work of God, a work that was commanded to be done; and it was of shedding blood, and of destroying the cities of Moab. For, saith he, "Cursed be he that keepeth back his sword from shedding of blood." As Saul, when he kept back the sword from shedding of blood at what time he was sent against Amaleck, was refused of God for being disobedient to God's commandment, in that he spared Agag the king. So that that place of the prophet was spoken of them that went to the destruction of the cities of Moab, among the which there was one called Nebo, which was much reproved for idolatry, superstition, pride, avarice, cruelty, tyranny, and for hardness of heart; and for these sins was plagued of God and destroyed.

Now what shall we say of these rich citizens of London? What shall I say of them? Shall I call them proud men of London, malicious men of London, merciless men of London? No, no, I may not say so; they will be offended with me then. Yet must I speak. For is there not reigning in London as much pride, as much covetousness, as much cruelty, as much oppression, and as much superstition, as was in Nebo? Yes, I think, and much more too. Therefore I say, repent, O London; repent, repent. Thou hearest thy faults told thee, amend them, amend them. . I think, if Nebo had had the preaching that thou hast, they would have converted. And, you rulers and officers, be wise and circumspect, look to your charge, and see you do your duties; and rather be glad to amend your ill living than to be angry when you are warned or told of your fault. What ado was there made in London at a certain man, because he said, (and indeed at that time on a just cause,) "Burgesses!" quoth he, "nay, Butterflies." Lord, what ado there was for that word! And yet would God they were no worse than butterflies! Butterflies do but their nature: the butterfly is not covetous, is not greedy, of other men's goods; is not full of envy and hatred, is not malicious, is not cruel, is not merciless. The butterfly glorieth not in her own deeds, nor preferreth the traditions of men before God's word; it committeth not idolatry, nor worshippeth false gods. But London cannot abide to be rebuked; such is the nature of man. If they be pricked, they will kick; if they be rubbed on the gall, they will wince; but yet they will not amend their faults, they will not be ill spoken of. But how shall I speak well of them?

If you could be content to receive and follow the word of God, and favour good preachers, if you could bear to be told of your faults, if you could amend when you hear of them, if you would be glad to reform that is amiss; if I might see any such inclination in you, that you would leave to be merciless, and begin to be charitable, I would then hope well of you, I would then speak well of you. But London was never so ill as it is now. In times past men were full of pity and compassion, but now there is no pity; for in London their brother shall die in the streets for cold, he shall lie sick at the door between stock and stock, I cannot tell what to call it, and perish there for hunger: was there ever more unmercifulness in Nebo? I think not. In times past, when any rich man died in London, they were wont to help the poor scholars of the Universities with exhibition. When any man died, they would bequeath great sums of money toward the relief of the poor. When I was a scholar in Cambridge myself, I heard very good report of London, and knew many that had relief of the rich men of London: but now I can hear no such good report, and yet I inquire of it, and hearken for it; but now charity is waxen cold, none helpeth the scholar, nor yet the poor. And in those days, what did they when they helped the scholars? Marry, they maintained and gave them livings that were very papists, and professed the pope's doctrine: and now that the knowledge of God's word is brought to light, and many earnestly study and labour to set it forth, now almost no man helpeth to maintain them.

Oh London, London! repent, repent; for I think God is more displeased with London than ever he was with the city of Nebo. Repent therefore, repent, London, and remember that the same God liveth now that punished Nebo, even the same God, and none other; and he will punish sin as well now as he did then: and he will punish the iniquity of London, as well as he did then of Nebo. Amend therefore. And ye that be prelates, look well to your office, for right prelating is busy labouring, and not lording. Therefore preach and teach, and let your plough be doing. Ye lords, I say, that live like loiterers, look well to your office; the plough is your office and charge. If you live idle and loiter, you do not your duty, you follow not your vocation: let your plough therefore be going, and not cease, that the ground may bring forth fruit.

But now methinketh I hear one say unto me: Wot ye what you say? Is it a work? Is it a labour? How then hath it happened that we have had so many hundred years so many unpreaching prelates, lording loiterers, and idle ministers? Ye would have me here to make answer, and to show cause thereof. Nay, this land is not for me to plough; it is too stony, too thorny, too hard for me to plough. They have so many things that make for them, so many things to lay for themselves, that it is not for my weak team to plough them. They have to lay for themselves long customs, ceremonies and authority, placing in parliament, and many things more. And I fear me this land is not yet ripe to be ploughed: for, as the saying is, it lacketh weathering: this gear lacketh weathering; at least way it is not for me to plough. For what shall I look for among thorns, but pricking and scratching? What among stones, but stumbling? What (I had almost said) among serpents, but stinging? But this much I dare say, that since lording and loitering hath come up, preaching hath come down, contrary to the apostles' times: for they preached and lorded not, and now they lord and preach not. For they that be lords will ill go to plough: it is no meet office for them; it is not seeming for their estate. Thus came up lording loiterers: thus crept in unpreaching prelates; and so have they long continued. For how many unlearned prelates have we now at this day! And no marvel: for if the ploughmen that now be were made lords, they would clean give over ploughing; they would leave off their labour, and fall to lording outright, and let the plough stand: and then both ploughs not walking, nothing should be in the commonweal but hunger.

For ever since the prelates were made lords and nobles, the plough standeth; there is no work done, the people starve. They hawk, they hunt, they card, they dice; they pastime in their prelacies with gallant gentlemen, with their dancing minions, and with their fresh companions, so that ploughing is set aside: and by their lording and loitering, preaching and ploughing is clean gone. And thus if the ploughmen of the country were as negligent in their office as prelates be, we should not long live, for lack of sustenance. And as it is necessary for to have this ploughing for the sustentation of the body, so must we have also the other for the satisfaction of the soul, or else we cannot live long ghostly. For as the body wasteth and consumeth away for lack of bodily meat, so doth the soul pine away for default of ghostly meat. But there be two kinds of inclosing, to let or hinder both these kinds of ploughing: the one is an inclosing to let or hinder the bodily ploughing, and the other to let or hinder the holiday-ploughing, the church-ploughing.

The bodily ploughing is taken in and inclosed through singular commodity. For what man will let go, or diminish his private commodity for a commonwealth? And who will sustain any damage for the respect of a public commodity? The other plough also no man is diligent to set forward, nor no man will hearken to it. But to hinder and let it all men's ears are open; yea, and a great many of this kind of ploughmen, which are very busy, and would seem to be very good workmen. I fear me some be rather mock-gospellers, than faithful ploughmen. I know many myself that profess the gospel, and live nothing thereafter. I know them, and have been conversant with some of them. I know them, and (I speak it with a heavy heart) there is as little charity and good living in them as in any other; according to that which Christ said in the gospel to the great number of people that followed him, as though they had had any earnest zeal to his doctrine, whereas indeed they had it not; *Non quia vidistis signa, sed quia comedistis de panibus.* "Ye follow me," saith he, "not because ye have seen the signs and miracles that I have done; but because ye have eaten the bread, and refreshed your bodies, therefore you follow me." So that I think many one now-a-days professeth the gospel for the living's sake, not for the love they bear to God's word. But they that will be true ploughmen must work faithfully for God's sake, for the edifying of their brethren. And as diligently as the husbandman plougheth for the sustentation of the body, so diligently must the prelates and ministers labour for the feeding of the soul: both the ploughs must still be going, as most necessary for man. And wherefore are magistrates ordained, but that the tranquillity of the commonweal may be confirmed, limiting both ploughs?

But now for the fault of unpreaching prelates, methink I could guess what might be said for excusing of them. They are so troubled with lordly living, they be so placed in palaces, crouched in courts, ruffling in their rents, dancing in their dominions, burdened with ambassages, pampering of their paunches, like a monk that maketh his jubilee; munching in their mangers, and moiling in their gay manors and mansions, and so troubled with loitering in their lordships, that they cannot attend it. They are otherwise occupied, some in king's matters, some are ambassadors, some of the privy council, some to furnish the court, some are lords of the parliament, some are presidents, and comptrollers of mints.

Well, well, is this their duty? Is this their office? Is this their calling? Should we have ministers of the church to be comptrollers of the mints? Is this a meet office for a priest that hath cure of souls? Is this his charge? I would here ask one question: I would fain know who controlleth the devil at home in his parish, while he controlleth the mint? If the apostles might not leave the office of preaching to the deacons, shall one leave it for minting? I cannot tell you; but the saying is, that since priests have been minters, money hath been worse than it was before. And they say that the evilness of money hath made all things dearer. And in this behalf I must speak to England. "Hear, my country, England," as Paul said in his first epistle to the Corinthians, the sixth chapter; for Paul was no sitting bishop, but a walking and a preaching bishop. But when he went from them, he left there behind him the plough going still; for he wrote unto them, and rebuked them for going to law, and pleading their causes before heathen judges: "Is there," said he, utterly among you no wise man, to be an arbitrator in matters of judgment? What, not one of all that can judge between brother and brother; but one brother goeth to law with another, and that under heathen judges? *Constituite contemptos qui sunt in ecclesia*, &c. Appoint them judges that are most abject and vile in the congregation." Which he speaketh in rebuking them; "For," saith he, *ad erubescentiam vestram dico*—"I speak it to your shame." So, England, I speak it to thy shame: is there never a nobleman to be a lord president, but it must be a prelate? Is there never a wise man in the realm to be a comptroller of the mint? I speak it to your shame. I speak it to your shame. If there be never a wise man, make a water-bearer, a tinker, a cobbler, a slave, a page, comptroller of the mint: make a mean gentleman, a groom, a yeoman, or a poor beggar, lord president.

Thus I speak, not that I would have it so; but "to your shame," if there be never a gentleman meet nor able to be lord president. For why are not the noblemen and young gentlemen of England so brought up in knowledge of God, and in learning, that they may be able to execute offices in the commonweal? The king hath a great many of wards, and I trow there is a Court of Wards: why is there not a school for the wards, as well as there is a Court for their lands? Why are they not set in schools where they may learn? Or why are they not sent to the universities, that they may be able to serve the king when they come to age? If the wards and young gentlemen were well brought up in learning, and in the knowledge of God, they would not when they come to age so much give themselves to other vanities. And if the nobility be well trained in godly learning, the people would follow the same train. For truly, such as the noblemen be, such will the people be. And now, the only cause why noblemen be not made lord presidents, is because they have not been brought up in learning.

Therefore for the love of God appoint teachers and schoolmasters, you that have charge of youth; and give the teachers stipends worthy their pains, that they may bring them up in grammar, in logic, in rhetoric, in philosophy, in the civil law, and in that which I cannot leave unspoken of, the word of God. Thanks be unto God, the nobility otherwise is very well brought up in learning and godliness, to the great joy and comfort of England; so that there is now good hope in the youth, that we shall another day have a flourishing commonweal, considering their godly education. Yea, and there be already noblemen enough, though not so many as I could wish, able to be lord presidents, and wise men enough for the mint. And as unmeet a thing it is for bishops to be lord presidents, or priests to be minters, as it was for the

Corinthians to plead matters of variance before heathen judges. It is also a slander to the noblemen, as though they lacked wisdom and learning to be able for such offices, or else were no men of conscience, or else were not meet to be trusted, and able for such offices. And a prelate hath a charge and cure otherwise; and therefore he cannot discharge his duty and be a lord president too. For a presidentship requireth a whole man; and a bishop cannot be two men. A bishop hath his office, a flock to teach, to look unto; and therefore he cannot meddle with another office, which alone requireth a whole man: he should therefore give it over to whom it is meet, and labour in his own business; as Paul writeth to the Thessalonians, "Let every man do his own business, and follow his calling." Let the priest preach, and the noblemen handle the temporal matters. Moses was a marvellous man, a good man: Moses was a wonderful fellow, and did his duty, being a married man: we lack such as Moses was. Well, I would all men would look to their duty, as God hath called them, and then we should have a flourishing christian commonweal.

And now I would ask a strange question: who is the most diligentest bishop and prelate in all England, that passeth all the rest in doing his office? I can tell, for I know him who it is; I know him well. But now I think I see you listening and hearkening that I should name him. There is one that passeth all the other, and is the most diligent prelate and preacher in all England. And will ye know who it is? I will tell you: it is the devil. He is the most diligent preacher of all other; he is never out of his diocess; he is never from his cure; ye shall never find him unoccupied; he is ever in his parish; he keepeth residence at all times; ye shall never find him out of the way, call for him when you will he is ever at home; the diligentest preacher in all the realm; he is ever at his plough: no lording nor loitering can hinder him; he is ever applying his business, ye shall never find him idle, I warrant you. And his office is to hinder religion, to maintain superstition, to set up idolatry, to teach all kind of popery. He is ready as he can be wished for to set forth his plough; to devise as many ways as can be to deface and obscure God's glory. Where the devil is resident, and hath his plough going, there away with books, and up with candles; away with bibles, and up with beads; away with the light of the gospel, and up with the light of candles, yea, at noon-days. Where the devil is resident, that he may prevail, up with all superstition and idolatry; censing, painting of images, candles, palms, ashes, holy water, and new service of men's inventing; as though man could invent a better way to honour God with than God himself hath appointed. Down with Christ's cross, up with purgatory pickpurse, up with him, the popish purgatory, I mean. Away with clothing the naked, the poor and impotent; up with decking of images, and gay garnishing of stocks and stones: up with man's traditions and his laws, down with God's traditions and his most holy word. Down with the old honour due to God, and up with the new god's honour. Let all things be done in Latin: there must be nothing but Latin, not so much as *Memento, homo, quod cinis es, et in cinerem reverteris:* "Remember, man, that thou art ashes, and into ashes thou shalt return:" which be the words that the minister speaketh unto the ignorant people, when he giveth them ashes upon Ash-Wednesday; but it must be spoken in Latin: God's word may in no wise be translated into English.

Oh that our prelates would be as diligent to sow the corn of good doctrine, as Satan is to sow cockle and darnel! And this is the devilish ploughing, the which worketh to have things in Latin, and letteth the fruitful edification. But here some man will say to me, What, sir, are ye so privy of the devil's counsel, that ye know all this to be true? Truly I know him too well, and have obeyed him a little too much in condescending to some follies; and I know him as other men do, yea, that he is ever occupied, and ever busy in following his plough. I know by St. Peter, which saith of him, *Sicut leo rugiens circuit quærens quem devoret:* "He goeth about like a roaring lion, seeking whom he may devour." I would have this text well viewed and examined, every word of it: "*Circuit,*" he goeth about in every corner of his diocess; he goeth on visitation daily, he leaveth no place of his cure unvisited: he walketh round about from place to place, and ceaseth not. "*Sicut leo,*" as a lion, that is, strongly, boldly, and proudly; stately and fiercely with haughty looks, with his proud countenances, with his stately braggings. "*Rugiens,*" roaring; for he letteth not slip any occasion to speak or to roar out when he seeth his time. "*Quærens,*" he goeth about seeking, and not sleeping, as our bishops do; but he seeketh diligently, he searcheth diligently all corners, where as he may have his prey. He roveth abroad in every place of his diocess; he standeth not still, he is never at rest, but ever in hand with his plough, that it may go forward. But there was never such a preacher in England as he is. Who is able to tell his diligent preaching, which every day, and every hour, laboureth to sow cockle and darnel, that he may bring out of form, and out of estimation and room, the institution of the Lord's supper, and Christ's cross? For there he lost his right; for Christ said, *Nunc judicium est mundi, princeps seculi hujus ejicietur foras. Et sicut exaltavit Moses serpentem in deserto, ita exaltari oportet Filium hominis. Et cum exaltatus fuero a terra, omnia traham ad meipsum.* "Now is the judgment of this world, and the prince of this world shall be cast out. And as Moses did lift up the serpent in the wilderness, so must the Son of man be lift up. And when I shall be lift up from the earth, I will draw all things unto myself." For the devil was disappointed of his purpose: for he thought all to be his own; and when he had once brought Christ to the cross, he thought all cocksure. But there lost he all reigning: for Christ said, *Omnia traham ad meipsum:* "I will draw all things to myself." He meaneth, drawing of man's soul to salvation. And that he said he would do *per semetipsum*, by his own self; not by any other body's sacrifice. He meant by his own sacrifice on the cross, where he offered himself for the redemption of mankind; and not the sacrifice of the mass to be offered by another. For who can offer him but himself? He was both the offerer and the offering. And this is the prick, this is the mark at the which the devil shooteth, to evacuate the cross of Christ, and to mingle the institution of the Lord's supper; the which although he cannot bring to pass, yet he goeth about by his sleights and subtil means to frustrate the same; and these fifteen hundred years he hath been a doer, only purposing to evacuate Christ's death, and to make it of small efficacy and virtue. For whereas Christ, according as the serpent was lifted up in the wilderness, so would he himself be exalted, that thereby as many as trusted in him should have salvation; but the devil would none of that: they would have us saved by a daily oblation propitiatory, by a sacrifice expiatory, or remissory.

Now if I should preach in the country, among the unlearned, I would tell what propitiatory, expiatory, and remissory is; but here is a learned auditory: yet for them that be unlearned I will expound it. Propitiatory, expiatory, remissory, or satisfactory, for they signify all one thing in effect, and is nothing else but a thing whereby to obtain remission of sins, and to have salvation. And this way the devil used to evacuate the death of Christ, that we might have affiance in other things, as in the sacrifice of the priest; whereas Christ would have us to trust in his only sacrifice. So he was, *Agnus occisus ab origine mundi;* "The Lamb that hath been slain from the beginning of the world;" and therefore he is called *juge sacrificium,* "a continual sacrifice;" and not for the continuance of the mass, as the blanchers have blanched it, and wrested it; and as I myself did once betake it. But Paul saith, *per semetipsum purgatio facta:* "By himself," and by none other, Christ "made purgation" and satisfaction for the whole world.

Would Christ this word, "by himself," had been better weighed and looked upon, and *in sanctificationem*, to make them holy; for he is *juge sacrificium*, " a continual sacrifice," in effect, fruit, and operation; that like as they, which seeing the serpent hang up in the desert, were put in remembrance of Christ's death, in whom as many as believed were saved; so all men that trusted in the death of Christ shall be saved, as well they that were before, as they that came after. For he was a continual sacrifice, as I said, in effect, fruit, operation, and virtue; as though he had from the beginning of the world, and continually should to the world's end, hang still on the cross; and he is as fresh hanging on the cross now, to them that believe and trust in him, as he was fifteen hundred years ago, when he was crucified.

Then let us trust upon his only death, and look for none other sacrifice propitiatory, than the same bloody sacrifice, the lively sacrifice; and not the dry sacrifice, but a bloody sacrifice. For Christ himself said, *consummatum est:* "It is perfectly finished: I have taken at my Father's hand the dispensation of redeeming mankind, I have wrought man's redemption, and have despatched the matter." Why then mingle ye him? Why do ye divide him? Why make you of him more sacrifices than one? Paul saith, *Pascha nostrum immolatus est Christus:* "Christ our passover is offered;" so that the thing is done, and Christ hath done it *semel*, once for all; and it was a bloody sacrifice, not a dry sacrifice. Why then, it is not the mass that availeth or profiteth for the quick and the dead.

Wo worth thee, O devil, wo worth thee, that hast prevailed so far and so long; that hast made England to worship false gods, forsaking Christ their Lord. Wo worth thee, devil, wo worth thee, devil, and all thy angels. If Christ by his death draweth all things to himself, and draweth all men to salvation, and to heavenly bliss, that trust in him; then the priests at the mass, at the popish mass, I say, what can they draw, when

Christ draweth all, but lands and goods from the right heirs? The priests draw goods and riches, benefices and promotions to themselves; and such as believed in their sacrifices they draw to the devil. But Christ is he that draweth souls unto him by his bloody sacrifice. What have we to do then but *epulari in Domino*, to eat in the Lord at his supper? What other service have we to do to him, and what other sacrifice have we to offer, but the mortification of our flesh? What other oblation have we to make, but of obedience, of good living, of good works, and of helping our neighbours? But as for our redemption, it is done already, it cannot be better: Christ hath done that thing so well, that it cannot be amended. It cannot be devised how to make that any better than he hath done it. But the devil, by the help of that Italian bishop yonder, his chaplain, hath laboured by all means that he might to frustrate the death of Christ and the merits of his passion. And they have devised for that purpose to make us believe in other vain things by his pardons; as to have remission of sins for praying on hallowed beads; for drinking of the bakehouse bowl; as a canon of Waltham Abbey once told me, that whensoever they put their loaves of bread into the oven, as many as drank of the pardon-bowl should have pardon for drinking of it. A mad thing, to give pardon to a bowl! Then to pope Alexander's holy water, to hallowed bells, palms, candles, ashes, and what not? And of these things, every one hath taken away some part of Christ's sanctification; every one hath robbed some part of Christ's passion and cross, and hath mingled Christ's death, and hath been made to be propitiatory and satisfactory, and to put away sin. Yea, and Alexander's holy water yet at this day remaineth in England, and is used for a remedy against spirits and to chase away devils; yea, and I would this had been the worst. I would this were the worst. But wo worth thee, O devil, that has prevailed to evacuate Christ's cross, and to mingle the Lord's supper. These be the Italian bishop's devices, and the devil hath pricked at this mark to frustrate the cross of Christ: he shot at this mark long before Christ came, he shot at it four thousand years before Christ hanged on the cross, or suffered his passion.

For the brasen serpent was set up in the wilderness, to put men in remembrance of Christ's coming; that like as they which beheld the brasen serpent were healed of their bodily diseases, so they that looked spiritually upon Christ that was to come, in him should be saved spiritually from the devil. The serpent was set up in memory of Christ to come; but the devil found means to steal away the memory of Christ's coming, and brought the people to worship the serpent itself, and to cense him, to honour him, and to offer to him, to worship him, and to make an idol of him. And this was done by the market-men that I told you of. And the clerk of the market did it for the lucre and advantage of his master, that thereby his honour might increase; for by Christ's death he could have but small worldly advantage. And so even now so hath he certain blanchers belonging to the market, to let and stop the light of the gospel, and to hinder the king's proceedings in setting forth the word and glory of God. And when the king's majesty, with the advice of his honourable council, goeth about to promote God's word, and to set an order in matters of religion, there shall not lack blanchers that will say, "As for images, whereas they have used to be censed, and to have candles offered unto to them, none be so foolish to do it to the stock or stone, or to the image itself; but it is done to God and his honour before the image." And though they should abuse it, these blanchers will be ready to whisper the king in the ear, and to tell him, that this abuse is but a small matter; and that the same, with all other like abuses in the church, may be reformed easily. "It is but a little abuse," say they, "and it may be easily amended. But it should not be taken in hand at the first, for fear of trouble or further inconveniences. The people will not bear sudden alterations; an insurrection may be made after sudden mutation, which may be to the great harm and loss of the realm. Therefore all things shall be well, but not out of hand, for fear of further business." These be the blanchers, that hitherto have stopped the word of God, and hindered the true setting forth of the same. There be so many put-offs, so many put-byes, so many respects and considerations of worldly wisdom: and I doubt not but there were blanchers in the old time to whisper in the ear of good king Hezekiah, for the maintenance of idolatry done to the brasen serpent, as well as there hath been now of late, and be now, that can blanch the abuse of images, and other like things. But good king Hezekiah would not be so blinded; he was like to Apollos, "fervent in spirit." He would give no ear to the blanchers; he was not moved with the worldly respects, with these prudent considerations, with these policies: he feared not insurrections of the people: he feared not lest his people would bear not the glory of God; but he, without any of these respects, or policies, or considerations, like a good king, for God's sake and for conscience sake, by and by plucked down the brasen serpent, and destroyed it utterly, and beat it to powder. He out of hand did cast out all images, he destroyed all idolatry, and clearly did extirpate all superstition. He would not hear these blanchers and worldly-wise men, but without delay followeth God's cause, and destroyeth all idolatry out of hand. Thus did good king Hezekiah; for he was like Apollos, fervent in spirit, and diligent to promote God's glory.

And good hope there is, that it shall be likewise here in England; for the king's majesty is so brought up in knowledge, virtue, and godliness, that it is not to be mistrusted but that we shall have all things well, and that the glory of God shall be spread abroad throughout all parts of the realm, if the prelates will diligently apply their plough, and be preachers rather than lords. But our blanchers, which will be lords, and no labourers, when they are commanded to go and be resident upon their cures, and preach in their benefices, they would say, "What? I have set a deputy there; I have a deputy that looketh well to my flock, and the which shall discharge my duty." "A deputy," quoth he! I looked for that word all this while. And what a deputy must he be, trow ye? Even one like himself: he must be a canonist; that is to say, one that is brought up in the study of the pope's laws and decrees; one that will set forth papistry as well as himself will do; and one that will maintain all superstition and idolatry; and one that will nothing at all, or else very weakly, resist the devil's plough: yea, happy it is if he take no part with the devil; and where he should be an enemy to him, it is well if he take not the devil's part against Christ.

But in the meantime the prelates take their pleasures. They are lords, and no labourers: but the devil is diligent at his plough. He is no unpreaching prelate: he is no lordly loiterer from his cure, but a busy ploughman; so that among all the prelates, and among all the pack of them that have cure, the devil shall go for my money, for he still applieth his business. Therefore, ye unpreaching prelates, learn of the devil: to be diligent in doing of your office, learn of the devil: and if you will not learn of God, nor good men, for shame learn of the devil; *ad erubescentiam vestrum dico*, "I speak it for your shame:" if you will not learn of God, nor good men, to be diligent in your office, learn of the devil. Howbeit there is now very good hope that the king's majesty, being of the help of good governance of his most honourable counsellors trained and brought up in learning, and knowledge of God's word, will shortly provide a remedy, and set an order herein; which thing that it may so be, let us pray for him. Pray for him, good people; pray for him. Ye have great cause and need to pray for him.

A SERMON ON THE PARABLE OF A KING THAT MARRIED HIS SON, MADE BY MASTER LATIMER.

Matthew XXII. [2, 3.]

Simile factum est regnum cœlorum homini regi qui fecit nuptias filio suo.

The kingdom of heaven is like unto a certain king, which married his son, and sent forth his servants to call them that, &c.

This is a gospel that containeth very much matter; and there is another like unto this in the fourteenth of Luke: but they be both one in effect, for they teach both one thing; and therefore I will take them both in hand together, because they tend to one purpose. Matthew saith, "The kingdom of heaven is like unto a certain king, which married his son;" Luke saith, "A certain man ordained a great supper:" but there is no difference in the very substance of the matter, for they pertain to one purpose. Here is made mention of a feast-maker: therefore we must consider who was the feast-maker: secondarily, who was his son: thirdly, we must consider to whom he was married: fourthly, who were they that called the guests : fifthly, who were the guests. And then we must know how the guest-callers behaved themselves: and then, how the guests behaved themselves towards them that called them. When all these circumstances be considered, we shall find much good matters covered and hid in this gospel.

Now that I may so handle these matters, that it may turn to the edification of your souls, and to the discharge of my office, I will most instantly desire you to lift up your hearts unto God, and desire his divine Majesty, in the name of his only-begotten Son, our Saviour Jesus Christ, that he will give unto us his Holy Ghost :—unto me, that I may speak the word of God, and teach you to understand the same ; unto you, that you may hear it fruitfully, to the edification of your souls ; so that you may be edified through it, and your lives reformed and amended ; and that his honour and glory may increase daily amongst us. Wherefore I shall desire you to say with me, " Our Father," &c.

Dearly beloved in the Lord, the gospel that is read this day is a parable, a similitude or comparison. For our Saviour compared the kingdom of God unto a man that made a marriage for his son. And here was a marriage. At a marriage, you know, there is commonly great feastings. Now you must know who was this feast-maker, and who was his son, and to whom he was married; and who were those that should be called, and who were the callers; how they behaved themselves, and how the guests behaved themselves towards them that called them.

Now this marriage-maker, or feast-maker, is Almighty God. Luke the Evangelist calleth him a man, saying, "A certain man ordained a great supper." He calleth him a man, not that he was incarnate, or hath taken our flesh upon him: no, not so; for you must understand that there be three Persons in the Deity, God the Father, God the Son, and God the Holy Ghost. And these three Persons decked the Son with manhood; so that neither the Father, neither the Holy Ghost, took flesh upon them, but only the Son; he took our flesh upon him, taking it of the Virgin Mary. But Luke called God the Father a man, not because he took flesh upon him, but only compared him unto a man; not that he will affirm him to be a man. Who was he now that was married? Who was the bridegroom? Marry, that was our Saviour Jesus Christ, the second person in the Deity; the eternal Son of God. Who should be his spouse? To whom was he married? To his church and congregation: for he would have all the world to come unto him, and to be married unto him: but we see by daily experience that the most part refuse his offer. But here is shewed the state of the church of God: for this marriage, this feast, was begun at the beginning of the world, and shall endure to the end of the same: yet for all that, the most part refused it: for at the very beginning of the world, ever the most part refused to come. And so it appeareth at this time, how little a number cometh to this wedding and feast: though we have callers, yet there be but few of those that come. So ye hear that God is the feast-maker; the bridegroom is Christ, his Son, our Saviour; the bride is the congregation.

Now what manner of meat was prepared at this great feast? For ye know it is commonly seen, that at a marriage the finest meat is prepared that can be gotten. What was the chiefest dish at this great banquet? What was the feast-dish? Marry, it was the bridegroom himself: for the Father, the feast-maker, prepared none other manner of meat for the guests, but the body and blood of his own natural Son. And this is the chiefest dish at this banquet; which truly is a marvellous thing, that the Father offereth his Son to be eaten. Verily, I think that no man hath heard the like. And truly there was never such kind of feasting as this is, where the Father will have his Son to be eaten, and his blood to be drunk.

We read in a story, that a certain man had eaten his son; but it was done unawares: he knew not that it was his son, else no doubt he would not have eaten him. The story is this:

There was a king named Astyages, which had heard by a prophecy, that one Cyrus should have the rule and dominion over his realm after his departure; which thing troubled the said king very sore, and therefore [he] sought all the ways and means how to get the said Cyrus out of the way; how to kill him, so that he should not be king after him. Now he had a nobleman in his house, named Harpagus, whom he appointed to destroy the said Cyrus: but howsoever the matter went, Cyrus was preserved and kept alive, contrary to the king's mind. Which thing when Astyages heard, what doth he? This he did: Harpagus, that nobleman which was put in trust to kill Cyrus, had a son in the court, whom the king commanded to be taken; his head, hands, and feet to be cut off; and his body to be prepared, roasted, or sodden, of the best manner as could be devised. After that, he biddeth Harpagus to come and eat with him, where there was jolly cheer; one dish coming after another. At length the king asked him, "Sir, how liketh you your fare?" Harpagus thanketh the king, with much praising the king's banquet. Now the king perceiving him to be merrily disposed, commanded one of his servants to bring in the head, hands, and feet of Harpagus's son. When it was done, the king showed him what manner of meat he had eaten, asking him how it liketh him. Harpagus made answer, though with an heavy heart, *Quod regi placet, id mihi quoque placet*; "Whatsoever pleaseth the king, that also pleaseth me." And here we have an ensample of a flatterer, or dissembler: for this Harpagus spake against his own heart and conscience. Surely, I fear me, there be a great many of flatterers in our time also, which will not be ashamed to speak against their own heart and consciences, like as this Harpagus did; which had, no doubt, a heavy heart, and in his conscience the act of the king misliked him, yet for all that, with his tongue he praised the same. So I say, we read not in any story, that at any time any father had eaten his son willingly and wittingly; and this Harpagus, of whom I rehearsed the story, did it unawares.

But the Almighty God, which prepared this feast for all the world, for all those that will come unto it, he offereth his only Son to be eaten, and his blood to be drunken. Belike he loved his guests well, because he did feed them with so costly a dish.

Again, our Saviour, the bridegroom, offereth himself at his last supper, which he had with his disciples, his body to be eaten, and his blood to be drunk. And to the intent that it should be done to our great comfort; and then again to take away all cruelty, irksomeness, and horribleness, he sheweth unto us how we shall eat him, in what manner and form; namely, spiritually, to our great comfort: so that whosoever eateth the mystical bread, and drinketh the mystical wine worthily, according to the ordinance of Christ, he receiveth surely the very body and blood of Christ spiritually, as it shall be most comfortable unto his soul. He eateth with the mouth of his soul, and digesteth with the stomach of his soul, the body of Christ. And to be short: whosoever believeth in Christ, putteth his hope, trust, and confidence in him, he eateth and drinketh him: for the spiritual eating is the right eating to everlasting life; not the corporal eating, as the Capernaites understood it. For that same corporal eating, on which they set their minds, hath no commodities at all; it is a spiritual meat that feedeth our souls.

But I pray you, how much is this supper of Christ regarded amongst us, where he himself exhibiteth unto us his body and blood? How much, I say, is it regarded? How many receive it with the curate or minister? O Lord, how blind and dull are we to such things, which pertain to our salvation! But I pray you, wherefore was it ordained principally? Answer: it was ordained for our help, to help our memory withal; to put us in mind of the great goodness of God, in redeeming us from everlasting death by the blood of our Saviour Christ; yea, and to signify unto us, that his body and blood is our meat and drink for our souls, to feed them to everlasting life. If we were now so perfect as we ought to be, we should not have need of it: but to help our imperfectness it was ordained of Christ; for we be so forgetful, when we be not pricked forward, we have soon forgotten all his benefits. Therefore to the intent that we might better keep it in memory, and to remedy this our slothfulness, our Saviour hath ordained this his supper for us, whereby we should remember his great goodness, his bitter passion and death, and so strengthen our faith: so that he instituted this supper for our sake, to make us to keep in fresh memory his inestimable benefits. But, as I said before, it is in a manner nothing regarded amongst us: we care not for it; we will not come unto it. How many be there, think ye, which regard this supper of the Lord as much as a testoon? But very few, no doubt of it: and I will prove that they regard it not so much. If there were a proclamation made in this town, that whosoever would come unto the church at such an hour, and there go to the communion with the curate, should have a testoon; when such a proclamation were made, I think, truly, all the town would come and celebrate the communion to get a testoon: but they will not come to receive the body and blood of Christ, the food and nourishment of their souls, to the augmentation and strength of their faith! Do they not more regard now a testoon than Christ? But the cause which letteth us from celebrating of the Lord's Supper, is this: we have no mind nor purpose to leave sin and wickedness, which maketh us not to come to this supper, because we be not ready nor meet to receive it. But I require you in God's behalf, leave your wickedness, that ye may receive it worthily, according to his institution. For this supper is ordained, as I told you before, for our sake, to our profits and commodities: for if we were perfect, we should not need this outward sacrament; but our Saviour, knowing our weakness and forgetfulness, ordained this supper to the augmentation of our faith, and to put us in remembrance of his benefits. But we will not come: there come no more at once, but such as give the holy loaves from house to house; which follow rather the custom than any thing else. Our Saviour Christ saith in the gospel of St. John,

Ego sum panis vivus, qui de cœlo descendi; "I am the living bread which came down from heaven." Therefore whosoever feedeth of our Saviour Christ, he shall not perish; death shall not prevail against him: his soul shall depart out of his body, yet death shall not get the victory over him; he shall not be damned. He that cometh to that marriage, to that banquet, death shall be unto him but an entrance or a door to everlasting life. *Panis quem ego dabo caro mea est;* "The bread that I will give is my flesh, which I will give for the life of the world." As many as will feed upon him, shall attain to everlasting life: they shall never die; they shall prevail against death; death shall not hurt them, because he hath lost his strength. If we would consider this, no doubt we would be more desirous to come to the communion than we be; we would not be so cold; we would be content to leave our naughty living, and come to the Lord's table.

Now ye have heard what shall be the chiefest dish at this marriage, namely, the body and blood of Christ. But now there be other dishes, which be sequels or hangings-on, wherewith the chief dish is powdered: that is, remission of sins; also the Holy Ghost, which ruleth and governeth our hearts; also the merits of Christ, which are made ours. For when we feed upon this dish worthily, then we shall have remission of our sins; we shall receive the Holy Ghost. Moreover, all the merits of Christ are ours; his fulfilling of the law is ours; and so we be justified before God, and finally attain to everlasting life. As many, therefore, as feed worthily of this dish, shall have all these things with it, and in the end everlasting life. St. Paul saith, *Qui proprio Filio suo non pepercit, sed pro nobis omnibus tradidit illum, quomodo non etiam cum illo omnia nobis donabit?* "He which spared not his own Son, but gave him for us all, how shall he not with him give us all things also?" Therefore they that be in Christ are partakers of all his merits and benefits; of everlasting life, and of all felicity. He that hath Christ hath all things that are Christ's. He is our preservation from damnation; he is our comfort; he is our help, our remedy. When we feed upon him, then we shall have remission of our sins: the same remission of sins is the greatest and most comfortable thing that can be in the world. O what a comfortable thing is this, when Christ saith, *Remittuntur tibi peccata*, "Thy sins are forgiven unto thee!" And this is a standing sentence; it was not spoken only to the same one man, but it is a general proclamation unto all us: all and every one that believeth in him shall have forgiveness of their sins. And this proclamation is cried out daily by his ministers and preachers; which proclamation is the word of grace, the word of comfort and consolation. For like as sin is the most fearful and the most horriblest thing in heaven and in earth, so the most comfortablest thing is the remedy against sin; which remedy is declared and offered unto us in this word of grace: and the power to distribute this remedy against sins he hath given unto his ministers, which be God's treasurers, distributers of the word of God. For now he speaketh by me, he calleth you to this wedding by me, being but a poor man; yet he hath sent me to call you. And though he be the author of the word, yet he will have men to be called through his ministers to that word. Therefore let us give credit unto the minister, when he speaketh God's word: yea, rather let us credit God when he speaketh by his ministers, and offereth us remission of our sins by his word. For there is no sin so great in this world, but it is pardonable as long as we be in this world, and call for mercy: for here is the time of mercy; here we may come to forgiveness of our sins. But if we once die in our sins and wickedness, so that we be damned, let us not look for remission afterwards: for the state after this life is unchangeable. But as long as we be here, we may cry for mercy. Therefore let us not despair: let us amend our lives, and cry unto God for forgiveness of our sins; and then no doubt we shall obtain remission, if we call with a faithful heart upon him, for so he hath promised unto us in his most holy word.

The holy scripture maketh mention of a sin against the Holy Ghost, which sin cannot be forgiven, neither in this world, nor in the world to come. And this maketh many men unquiet in their hearts and consciences: for some there be which ever be afraid, lest they have committed that same sin against the Holy Ghost, which is irremissible. Therefore some say, "I cannot tell whether I have sinned against the Holy Ghost or not: if I have committed that sin, I know I shall be damned." But I tell you what ye shall do: despair not of the mercy of God, for it is immeasurable. I cannot deny but that there is a sin against the Holy Ghost, which is irremissible: but we cannot judge of it aforehand, we cannot tell which man hath committed that sin or not, as long as he is alive; but when he is once gone, then I can judge whether he sinned against the Holy Ghost or not. As now I can judge that Nero, Saul, and Judas, and such like, that died in sins and wickedness, did commit this sin against the Holy Ghost: for they were wicked, and continued in their wickedness still to the very end; they made an end in their wickedness. But we cannot judge whether one of us sin this sin against the Holy Ghost, or not; for though a man be wicked at this time, yet he may repent, and leave his wickedness to-morrow, and so not commit that sin against the Holy Ghost. Our Saviour Christ pronounced against the scribes and Pharisees, that they had committed that sin against the Holy Ghost; because he knew their hearts, he knew they would still abide in their wickedness to the very end of their lives. But we cannot pronounce this sentence against any man, for we know not the hearts of men: he that sinneth now, peradventure shall be turned to-morrow, and leave his sins, and so be saved. Further, the promises of our Saviour Christ are general; they pertain to all mankind: he made a general proclamation, saying, *Qui credit in me, habet vitam æternam;* "Whosoever believeth in me hath everlasting life." Likewise St. Paul saith, *Gratia exsuperat supra peccatum;* "The grace and mercies of God exceedeth far our sins." Therefore let us ever think and believe that the grace of God, his mercy and goodness, exceedeth our sins. Also consider what Christ saith with his own mouth: *Venite ad me, omnes qui laboratis, &c.* "Come unto me, all ye that labour and are laden, and I will ease you." Mark, here he saith, "Come all ye:" wherefore then should any body despair, or shut out himself from these promises of Christ, which be general, and pertain to the whole world? For he saith, "Come all unto me." And then again he saith, *Refocillabo vos,* "I will refresh you:" you shall be eased from the burdens of your sins. Therefore, as I said before, he that is blasphemous, and obstinately wicked, and abideth in his wickedness still to the very end, he sinneth against the Holy Ghost; as St. Augustine, and all other godly writers do affirm. But he that leaveth his wickedness and sins, is content to amend his life, and then believing in Christ, seeketh salvation and everlasting life by him, no doubt that man or woman, whosoever he or they be, shall be saved: for they feed upon Christ, upon that meat that God the Father, this feast-maker, hath prepared for all his guests.

You have heard now who is the maker of this feast or banquet : and again, you have heard what meat is prepared for the guests ; what a costly dish the house-father hath ordained at the wedding of his son. But now ye know, that where there be great dishes and delicate fare, there be commonly prepared certain sauces, which shall give men a great lust and appetite to their meats ; as mustard, vinegar, and such like sauces. So this feast, this costly dish, hath its sauces ; but what be they ? Marry, the cross, affliction, tribulation, persecution, and all manner of miseries : for, like as sauces make lusty the stomach to receive meat, so affliction stirreth up in us a desire to Christ. For when we be in quietness, we are not hungry, we care not for Christ : but when we be in tribulation, and cast in prison, then we have a desire to him ; then we learn to call upon him ; then we hunger and thirst after him ; then we are desirous to feed upon him. As long as we be in health and prosperity, we care not for him ; we be slothful, we have no stomach at all ;

and therefore these sauces are very necessary for us. We have a common saying amongst us, when we see a fellow sturdy, lofty, and proud, men say, "This is a saucy fellow;" signifying him to be a high-minded fellow, which taketh more upon him than he ought to do, or his estate requireth: which thing, no doubt, is naught and ill; for every one ought to behave himself according unto his calling and estate. But he that will be a christian man, that intendeth to come to heaven, must be a saucy fellow; he must be well powdered with the sauce of affliction, and tribulation; not with proudness and stoutness, but with miseries and calamities: for so it is written, *Omnes qui pie volunt vivere in Christo persecutionem patientur;* "Whosoever will live godly in Christ, he shall have persecution and miseries:" he shall have sauce enough to his meat. Again, our Saviour saith, *Qui vult meus esse discipulus, abneget semetipsum et tollat crucem suam et sequatur me;* "He that will be my disciple must deny himself and take his cross upon him, and follow me."

Is there any man that will feed upon me, that will eat my flesh and drink my blood? Let him forsake himself. O this is a great matter; this is a biting thing, the denying of my own will! As for an ensample: I see a fair woman, and conceive in my heart an ill appetite to commit lechery with her; I desire to fulfil my wanton lust with her. Here is my appetite, my lust, my will: but what must I do? Marry, I must deny myself, and follow Christ. What is that? I must not follow my own desire, but the will and pleasure of Christ. Now what saith he? *Non fornicaberis, non adulteraberis;* "Thou shalt not be a whoremonger, thou shalt not be a wedlock-breaker." Here I must deny myself, and my will, and give place unto his will; abhor and hate my own will. Yea, and furthermore I must earnestly call upon him, that he will give me grace to withstand my own lust and appetite, in all manner of things which may be against his will: as when a man doth me wrong, taketh my living from me, or hurteth me in my good name and fame, my will is to avenge myself upon him, to do him a foul turn again; but what saith God? *Mihi vindicta, ego retribuam;* "Unto me belongeth vengeance, I will recompense the same." Now here I must give over my own will and pleasure, and obey his will: this I must do, if I will feed upon him, if I will come to heaven. But this is a bitter thing, a sour sauce, a sharp sauce; this sauce maketh a stomach: for when I am injured or wronged, or am in other tribulation, then I have a great desire for him, to feed upon him, to be delivered from trouble, and to attain to quietness and joy.

There is a learned man which hath a saying which is most true: he saith, *Plus crux quam tranquillitas invitat ad Christum;* "The cross and persecution bring us sooner to Christ than prosperity and wealth." Therefore St. Peter saith, *Humiliamini sub potenti manu Dei;* "Humble yourselves under the mighty hand of God." Look, what God layeth upon you, bear it willingly and humbly. But you will say, "I pray you, tell me what is my cross?" Answer: This that God layeth upon you, that same is your cross; not that which you of your own wilfulness lay upon yourselves: as there was a certain sect which were called Flagellarii, which scourged themselves with whips till the blood ran from their bodies; this was a cross, but it was not the cross of God. No, no: he laid not that upon them, they did it of their own head. Therefore look, what God layeth upon me, that same is my cross, which I ought to take in good part; as when I fall in poverty, or in miseries, I ought to be content withal; when my neighbour doth me wrong, taketh away my goods, robbeth me of my good name and fame, I shall bear it willingly, considering that it is God's cross, and that nothing can be done against me without his permission. There falleth never a sparrow to the ground without his permission; yea, not a hair falleth from our head without his will. Seeing then that there is nothing done without his will, I ought to bear this cross which he layeth upon me willingly, without any murmuring or grudging.

But I pray you, consider these words of St. Peter

well: *Humiliamini sub potenti manu Dei;* "Humble yourselves under the mighty hand of God." Here St. Peter signifieth unto us that God is a mighty God, which can take away the cross from us when it seemeth him good; yea, and he can send patience in the midst of all trouble and miseries. St. Paul, that elect instrument of God, shewed a reason wherefore God layeth afflictions upon us, saying: *Corripimur a Domino, ne cum mundo condemnemur;* "We are chastened of the Lord, lest we should be condemned with the world." For you see by daily experience, that the most part of wicked men are lucky in this world; they bear the swing, all things goeth after their minds; for God letteth them have their pleasures here. And therefore this is a common saying, "The more wicked, the more lucky:" but they that pertain to God, that shall inherit everlasting life, they must go to the pot; they must suffer here, according to that scripture, *Judicium a domo Dei incipit;* "The judgment of God beginneth at the house of God." Therefore it cometh of the goodness of God, when we be put to taste the sauce of tribulation: for he doth it to a good end, namely, that we should not be condemned with this wicked world. For these sauces are very good for us; for they make us more hungry and lusty to come to Christ and feed upon him. And truly, when it goeth well with us, we forget Christ, our hearts and minds are not upon him: therefore it is better to have affliction than to be in prosperity. For there is a common saying, *Vexatio dat intellectum;* "Vexation giveth understanding." David, that excellent king and prophet, saith, *Bonum est mihi quod humiliasti me, Domine:* "Lord," saith he, "it is good for me that thou hast pulled down my stomach, that thou hast humbled me." But I pray you, what sauce had David, how was he humbled? Truly thus: his own son defiled his daughter. After that, Absalom, one other of his sons, killed his own brother. And this was not enough, but his own son rose up against him, and traitorously cast him out of his kingdom, and defiled his wives in the sight of all the people. Was not he vexed? had he not sauces? Yes, yes: yet for all that he cried not out against God; he murmured not, but saith, *Bonum est mihi quod humiliasti me;* "Lord, it is good for me that thou hast humbled me, that thou hast brought me low." Therefore when we be in trouble, let us be of good comfort, knowing that God doth it for the best. But for all that, the devil, that old serpent, the enemy of mankind, doth what he can day and night to bring us this sauce, to cast us into persecution, or other miseries: as it appeareth in the gospel of Matthew, where our Saviour casting him out of a man, seeing that he could do no more harm, he desired Christ to give him leave to go into the swine; and so he cast them all into the sea. Where it appeareth, that the devil studieth and seeketh all manner of ways to hurt us, either in soul, or else in body. But for all that, let us not despair, but rather lift up our hearts unto God, desiring his help and comfort; and no doubt, when we do so, he will help: he will either take away the calamities, or else mitigate them, or at the leastwise send patience into our hearts, that we may bear it willingly.

Now you know, at a great feast, when there is made a delicate dinner, and the guests fare well, at the end of the dinner they have *bellaria*, certain subtleties, custards, sweet and delicate things: so when we come to this dinner, to this wedding, and feed upon Christ, and take his sauces which he hath prepared for us, at the end cometh the sweetmeat. What is that? Marry, remission of sins, and everlasting life; such joy, that no tongue can express, nor heart can think, which God hath prepared for all them that come to this dinner, and feed upon his Son, and taste of his sauces. And this is the end of this banquet. This banquet, or marriage-dinner, was made at the very beginning of the world. God made this marriage in paradise, and called the whole world unto it, saying, *Semen mulieris conteret caput serpentis;* "The Seed of the woman shall vanquish the head of the serpent." This was the first calling; and this calling stood unto the faithful in as good stead as it doth unto us, which have a more manifest calling. Afterward Almighty God called again with these words, speaking to Abraham: *Ego ero Deus tuus et seminis tui post te;* "I will be thy God, and thy seed's after thee." Now what is it to be our God? Forsooth to be our defender, our comforter, our deliverer, and helper. Who was Abraham's seed? Even Christ the Son of God, he was Abraham's seed: in him, and through him, all the world shall be blessed; all that believe in him, all that come to this dinner, and feed upon him. After that, all the prophets, their only intent was to call the people to this wedding. Now after the time was expired which God had appointed, he said, *Venite, parata sunt omnia;* "Come, all things are ready."

But who are these callers? The first was John Baptist, which not only called with his mouth, but also shewed with his finger that meat which God had prepared for the whole world. He saith, *Ecce Agnus Dei qui tollit peccata mundi;* "Lo, the Lamb of God, that taketh away the sins of the world." Also Christ himself called, saying, *Venite ad me, omnes qui laboratis;* "Come to me, all ye that travail and labour, and I will refresh you."

Likewise the apostles cried, and called all the whole world; as it is written, *Exivit sonus eorum per universam terram;* "Their sound is gone throughout all the world." But, I pray you, what thanks had they for their calling, for their labour? Verily this: John Baptist was beheaded; Christ was crucified; the apostles were killed: this was their reward for their labours. So all the preachers shall look for none other reward: for no doubt they must be sufferers, they must taste of these sauces: their office is, *arguere mundum de peccato,* "to rebuke the world of sin;" which no doubt is a thankless occupation. *Ut audiant montes judicia Domini,* "That the high hills," that is, great princes and lords, "may hear the judgments of the Lord:" they must spare no body; they must rebuke high and low, when they do amiss; they must strike them with the sword of God's word: which no doubt is a thankless occupation; yet it must be done, for God will have it so.

There be many men, which be not so cruel as to persecute or to kill the preachers of God's word;

but when they be called to feed upon Christ, to come to this banquet, to leave their wicked livings, then they begin to make their excuses; as it appeared here in this gospel, where " the first said, I have bought a farm, and I must needs go and see it; I pray thee have me excused. Another said, I have bought five yoke of oxen, and I go to prove them; I pray thee have me excused. The third said, I have married a wife, and therefore I cannot come." And these were their excuses. You must take heed that you mistake not this text: for after the outward letter it seemeth as though no husbandman, no buyer or seller, nor married man shall enter the kingdom of God. Therefore ye must take heed that ye understand it aright. For to be a husbandman, to be a buyer or seller, to be a married man, is a good thing, and allowed of God: but the abuse of such things is reproved. Husbandman, and married man, every one in his calling, may use and do the works of his calling. The husbandman may go to plough; they may buy and sell; also, men may marry; but they may not set their hearts upon it. The husbandman may not so apply his husbandry to set aside the hearing of the word of God; for when he doth so, he sinneth damnably: for he more regardeth his husbandry than God and his word; he hath all lust and pleasure in his husbandry, which pleasure is naught. As there be many husbandmen which will not come to service; they make their excuses that they have other business: but this excusing is naught; for commonly they go about wicked matters, and yet they would excuse themselves, to make themselves faultless; or, at the least way, they will diminish their faults, which thing itself is a great wickedness; to do wickedly, and then to defend that same wickedness, to neglect and despise God's word, and then to excuse such doings, like as these men do here in this gospel. The husbandman saith, "I have bought a farm; therefore have me excused: the other saith, I have bought five yoke of oxen; I pray thee have me excused:" Now when he cometh to the married man, that same fellow saith not, " Have me excused," as the others say; but he only saith, "I cannot come." Where it is to be noted, that the affections of carnal lusts and concupiscence are the strongest above all the other: for there be some men which set all their hearts upon voluptuousness; they regard nothing else, neither God nor his word; and therefore this married man saith, "I cannot come;" because his affections are more strong and more vehement than the other men's were.

But what shall be their reward which refuse to come? The house-father saith, "I say unto you, that none of those men which were bidden shall taste of my supper." With these words Christ our Saviour teacheth us, that all those that love better worldly things than God and his word shall be shut out from his supper; that is to say, from everlasting joy and felicity: for it is a great matter to despise God's word, or the minister of the same; for the office of preaching is the office of salvation; it hath warrants in scripture, it is grounded upon God's word. St. Paul to the Romans maketh a gradation of such-wise: *Omnis quicunque invo-*

caverit nomen Domini salvabitur: quomodo ergo invocabunt in quem non crediderunt, aut quomodo credent ei quem non audierunt? that is to say, "Whosoever shall call on the name of the Lord, shall be saved: but how shall they call upon him, in whom they believe not? How shall they believe on him of whom they have not heard? How shall they hear without a preacher? And how shall they preach, except they be sent?" At the length he concludeth, saying, *Fides ex auditu;* "Faith cometh by hearing." Where ye may perceive, how necessary a thing it is to hear God's word, and how needful a thing it is to have preachers, which may teach us the word of God: for by hearing we must come to faith; through faith we must be justified. And therefore Christ saith himself, *Qui credit in me, habet vitam æternam;* "He that believeth in me hath everlasting life." When we hear God's word by the preacher, and believe that same, then we shall be saved: for St. Paul saith, *Evangelium est potentia Dei ad salutem omni credenti;* "The gospel is the power of God unto salvation to all that believe; the gospel preached is God's power to salvation of all believers." This is a great commendation of this office of preaching: therefore we ought not to despise it, or little regard it; for it is God's instrument, whereby he worketh faith in our hearts. Our Saviour saith to Nicodeme, *Nisi quis renatus fuerit*, "Except a man be born anew, he cannot see the kingdom of God." But how cometh this regeneration? By hearing and believing of the word of God: for so saith St. Peter, *Renati non ex semine mortali corruptibili;* "We are born anew, not of mortal seed, but of immortal, by the word of God." Likewise Paul saith in another place, *Visum est Deo per stultitiam prædicationis salvos facere credentes;* "It pleased God to save the believers through the foolishness of preaching." But, peradventure, you will say, "What, shall a preacher teach foolishness?" No, not so: the preacher, when he is a right preacher, he preacheth not foolishness, but he preacheth the word of God; but it is taken for foolishness, the world esteemeth it for a trifle : but howsoever the world esteemeth it, St. Paul saith that God will save his through it.

Here I might take occasion to inveigh against those which little regard the office of preaching; which are wont to say, " What need we such preachings every day? Have I not five wits? I know as well what is good or ill, as he doth that preacheth." But I tell thee, my friend, be not too hasty ; for when thou hast nothing to follow but thy five wits, thou shalt go to the devil with them. David, that holy prophet, said not so : he trusted not his five wits, but he said, *Lucerna pedibus meis verbum tuum, Domine;* " Lord, thy word is a lantern unto my feet." Here we learn not to despise the word of God, but highly to esteem it, and reverently to hear it; for the holy day is ordained and appointed to none other thing, but that we should at that day hear the word of God, and exercise ourselves in all godliness. But there be some which think that this day is ordained only for feasting, drinking, or gaming, or such foolishness ; but they be much deceived : this day was appointed of God that we should hear his word, and learn his laws, and so serve him. But I dare say the devil hath no days so much service as upon Sundays or holy days; which Sundays are appointed to preaching, and to hear God's most holy word. Therefore God saith not only in his commandments, that we shall abstain from working; but he saith, *Sanctificabis,* "Thou shalt hallow:" so that holy day keeping is nothing else but to abstain from good works, and to do better works; that is, to come together, and celebrate the Communion together, and visit the sick bodies. These are holy-day works; and for that end God commanded us to abstain from bodily works, that we might be more meet and apt to do those works which he hath appointed unto us, namely, to feed our souls with his word, to remember his benefits, and to give him thanks, and to call upon him. So that the holy-day may be called a marriage-day, wherein we are married unto God; which day is very needful to be kept. The foolish common people think it to be a belly-cheer day, and so they make it a surfeiting day: there is no wickedness, no rebellion, no lechery, but she hath most commonly her beginning upon the holy-day.

We read a story in the fifteenth chapter of the book of Numbers, that there was a fellow which gathered sticks upon the sabbath-day; he was a despiser of God's ordinances and laws, like as they that now-a-days go about other business, when they should hear the word of God, and come to the Common Prayer: which fellows truly have need of sauce, to be made more lustier to come and feed upon Christ than they be. Now Moses and the people consulted with the Lord, what they should do, how they should punish that fellow which had so transgressed the sabbath-day. "He shall die," saith God: which thing is an ensample for us to take heed, that we transgress not the law of the sabbath-day. For though God punish us not by and by, as this man was punished; yet he is the very self-same God that he was before, and will punish one day, either here, or else in the other world, where the punishment shall be everlasting.

Likewise in the seventeenth chapter of the prophet Jeremy God threateneth his fearful wrath and anger unto those which do profane his sabbath-day. Again, he promiseth his favour and all prosperity to them that will keep the holy-days; saying, "Princes and kings shall go through thy gates," that is to say, Thou shalt be in prosperity, in wealth, and great estimation amongst thy neighbours. Again : " If ye will not keep my sabbath-day, I will kindle a fire in your gates ; " that is to say, I will destroy you, I will bring you to nought, and burn your cities with fire. These words pertain as well unto us at this time, as they pertained to them at their time : for God hateth the disallowing of the sabbath as well now as then ; for he is and remaineth still the old God : he will have us to keep his sabbath, as well now as then : for upon the sabbath-day God's seed-plough goeth ; that is to say, the ministry of his word is executed ; for the ministering of God's word is God's plough. Now upon the Sundays God sendeth his husbandmen to come and till; he sendeth his callers to come and call to the wedding, to bid the guests; that is, all the world to come to that supper. Therefore, for the reverence of God, consider these things: consider who calleth, namely, God; consider again who be the guests; all ye. Therefore I call you in God's name, come to this supper; hallow the sabbath-day; that is, do your holy-day work, come to this supper; for this day was appointed of God to that end, that his word should be taught and heard. Prefer not your own business therefore before the hearing of the word of God. Remember the story of that man which gathered sticks upon the holy day, and was put to death by the consent of God: where God shewed himself not a cruel God, but he would give warning unto the whole world by that man, that all the world should keep holy his sabbath-day.

The almighty ever-living God give us grace to live so in this miserable world, that we may at the end come to the great sabbath-day, where there shall be everlasting joy and gladness! *Amen.*

In Weekly Volumes, price **3d.** each.
(*Or in cloth, 6d. each.*)

CASSELL'S NATIONAL LIBRARY.

EDITED BY HENRY MORLEY, LL.D.,
Professor of English Literature at University College, London.

Volumes already published.

Warren Hastings	By LORD MACAULAY.
My Ten Years' Imprisonment (Memoirs of Silvio Pellico)	Translated from the Italian by THOMAS ROSCOE.
The Rivals, and The School for Scandal	By RICHARD BRINSLEY SHERIDAN.
The Autobiography of Benjamin Franklin.	
The Complete Angler	By ISAAC WALTON.
Childe Harold	By LORD BYRON.
The Man of Feeling	By HENRY MACKENZIE.
Sermons on the Card	By BISHOP LATIMER.

List of some of the Volumes to be published weekly.

Lives of Alexander the Great and Cæsar	By PLUTARCH.
The Castle of Otranto	By HORACE WALPOLE.
Voyages and Travels	By SIR JOHN MAUNDEVILLE
She Stoops to Conquer, and The Good-Natured Man	By OLIVER GOLDSMITH.
The Adventures of Baron Trenck	Translated from the German by THOMAS HOLCROFT.
Natural History of Selborne	By GILBERT WHITE.
Travels in the Interior of Africa	By MUNGO PARK.
The Wisdom of the Ancients	By LORD BACON.
Table-Talk	By MARTIN LUTHER.
The History of Egypt	By HERODOTUS.
A Voyage Round the World	By LORD ANSON.
Selected Voyages	From RICHARD HAKLUYT'S COLLECTION.
The Christian Year	By JOHN KEBLE.
Selected Philosophical Writings	By LORD BOLINGBROKE.
Thoughts on the Present Discontents	By EDMUND BURKE.
The History of Europe During the Middle Ages	By HENRY HALLAM.

CASSELL & COMPANY, LIMITED, *Ludgate Hill, London.*

Lat. Ser.]

# Selections from Bibles and Religious Works
Published by CASSELL & COMPANY.

Life of Christ, The. By the Ven. Archdeacon FARRAR, D.D., F.R.S.
    ILLUSTRATED EDITION, with about 300 Original Illustrations. 4to, cloth, 21s.; morocco antique, 42s.
    LIBRARY EDITION. Two Vols. Cloth, 24s.; morocco, 42s.
    BIJOU EDITION. Five Volumes, in box, 10s. 6d. the set.
    POPULAR EDITION. Cloth, 6s.; cloth, gilt edges, 7s. 6d.; Persian morocco, gilt edges, 10s. 6d.; tree-calf, 15s.

St. Paul, The Life and Work of. By the Ven. Archdeacon FARRAR, D.D., F.R.S.
    LIBRARY EDITION. Two Vols., cloth, 24s.; morocco, 42s.
    ILLUSTRATED EDITION. With about 300 Illustrations, £1 1s.; morocco, £2 2s.
    POPULAR EDITION. Cloth, 6s.; cloth, gilt edges, 7s. 6d.; Persian morocco, 10s. 6d.; tree-calf, 15s.

Early Days of Christianity, The. By the Ven. Archdeacon FARRAR, D.D., F.R.S.
    LIBRARY EDITION. Two Vols., 24s.; morocco, £2 2s.
    POPULAR EDITION. Cloth, 6s.; cloth, gilt edges, 7s. 6d.; Persian morocco, 10s. 6d.; tree-calf, 15s.

Moses and Geology; or, the Harmony of the Bible with Science. By SAMUEL KINNS, Ph.D., F.R.A.S. *New and Cheaper Edition.* Illustrated, 6s.

Bible, The Crown. Illustrated. With about 1,000 Original Illustrations. With References. &c. Cloth, 7s. 6d.

Bible, Cassell's Illustrated Family. With 900 Illustrations. Leather, gilt edges, £2 10s.

Bible Dictionary, Cassell's. With nearly 600 Illustrations. 7s. 6d.

Bible Educator, The. Edited by the Very Rev. Dean PLUMPTRE, D.D. With Illustrations. Four Vols., cloth, 6s. each.

Bunyan's Pilgrim's Progress (Cassell's). Demy 4to. Illustrated throughout. 7s. 6d. *Popular Edition,* 3s. 6d.

Bunyan's Holy War. With 100 Illustrations. 10s. 6d.

Child's Life of Christ, The. With about 200 Original Illustrations. 21s.

Child's Bible, The. With 200 Illustrations. 143rd *Thousand. Cheap Edition,* 7s. 6d.

Church at Home, The. A Series of Short Sermons. By the Rt. Rev. ROWLEY HILL, D.D., Bishop of Sodor and Man. 5s.

Commentary, The New Testament, for English Readers. Edited by the Rt. Rev. C. J. ELLICOTT, D.D., Lord Bishop of Gloucester and Bristol. In 3 Vols., 21s. each.

Commentary, The Old Testament, for English Readers. Edited by the Rt. Rev. C. J. ELLICOTT, D.D., Lord Bishop of Gloucester and Bristol. Complete in 5 Vols., 21s. each.

Difficulties of Belief, Some. By the Rev. T. TEIGNMOUTH SHORE, M.A. *Cheap Edition.* 2s. 6d.

Doré Bible. With 230 Illustrations by GUSTAVE DORÉ. 2 Vols., cloth, £2 10s.; Persian morocco, £3 10s.; Original Edition, 2 Vols., cloth, £8.

Family Prayer-Book, The. Edited by Rev. Canon GARBETT, M.A., and Rev. S. MARTIN. Cloth, 5s.; morocco, 18s.

Selections from Cassell & Company's Publications (continued).

Geikie, Cunningham, D.D., Works by :—
- **Hours with the Bible.** Six Vols., 6s.
- **Entering on Life.** 3s. 6d.
- **The Precious Promises.** 2s. 6d.
- **The English Reformation.** 5s.
- **Old Testament Characters.** 6s.
- **The Life and Words of Christ.** Two Vols., cloth, 30s. *Students' Edition*, Two Vols., 16s.

Glories of the Man of Sorrows, The. Sermons preached at St. James's, Piccadilly. By the Rev. H. G. BONAVIA HUNT. 2s. 6d.

"Heart Chords." A Series of Works by Eminent Divines. Bound in cloth, red edges. One Shilling each.
- **My Father.** By the Right Rev. ASHTON OXENDEN, late Bishop of Montreal.
- **My Bible.** By the Right Rev. W. BOYD CARPENTER, Bishop of Ripon.
- **My Work for God.** By the Right Rev. Bishop COTTERILL.
- **My Object in Life.** By the Ven. Archdeacon FARRAR.
- **My Aspirations.** By the Rev. G. MATHESON, D.D.
- **My Emotional Life.** By the Rev. Preb. CHADWICK, D.D.
- **My Body.** By the Rev. Prof. W. G. BLAIKIE, D.D.
- **My Soul.** By the Rev. P. B. POWER, M.A.
- **My Growth in Divine Life.** By the Rev. Prebendary REYNOLDS, M.A.
- **My Hereafter.** By the Very Rev. Dean BICKERSTETH.
- **My Walk with God.** By the Very Rev. Dean MONTGOMERY.
- **My Aids to the Divine Life.** By Very Rev. Dean BOYLE.
- **My Sources of Strength.** By the Rev. E. E. JENKINS, M.A., Secretary of the Wesleyan Missionary Society.

Marriage Ring, The. By WILLIAM LANDELS, D.D. Bound in white leatherette, gilt edges, in box, 6s.; morocco, 8s. 6d.

Martyrs, Foxe's Book of. With about 200 Illustrations. Cloth, 12s.; cloth gilt, gilt edges, 15s.

Music of the Bible, The. By J. STAINER, M.A., Mus.Doc. 2s. 6d.

Near and the Heavenly Horizons, The. By the Countess DE GASPARIN. 1s.; cloth, 2s.

Patriarchs, The. By the late Rev. W. HANNA, D.D., and the Ven. Archdeacon NORRIS, B.D. 2s. 6d.

Protestantism, The History of. By the Rev. J. A. WYLIE, LL.D. Containing upwards of 600 Original Illustrations. Three Vols., 27s.; Library Edition, 30s.

Quiver Yearly Volume, The. With 250 high-class Illustrations. 7s. 6d.

Sacred Poems, The Book of. Edited by the Rev. Canon BAYNES, M.A. With Illustrations. Cloth, gilt edges, 5s.

St. George for England; and other Sermons preached to Children. By the Rev. T. TEIGNMOUTH SHORE, M.A. 5s.

Sermons Preached at Westminster Abbey. By ALFRED BARRY, D.D., L.C.L., Primate of Australia. 5s.

Shall We Know One Another? By the Rt. Rev. J. C. RYLE, D.D., Bishop of Liverpool. *New and Enlarged Edition.* 1s.

Simon Peter: His Life, Times, and Friends. By E. HODDER. 5s.

Voice of Time, The. By JOHN STROUD. Cloth gilt, 1s.

CASSELL & COMPANY, LIMITED, *Ludgate Hill, London.*

CASSELL & COMPANY'S
Monthly Serial Publications.*

A List of these is subjoined in alphabetical order, with a note of the price at which they are published monthly.

Art, Magazine of. 1s.
Bible Work at Home and Abroad. 2d.
British Ballads. 7d.
British Battles. 7d.
Butterflies and Moths, European. 6d.
Canaries and Cage-Birds. 6d.
Cassell's Magazine. 7d.
Child's Life of Christ. 7d.
Christian Worker, The. 1d.
Cookery, Cassell's Dictionary of. 6d.
Countries of the World. 7d.
Doré Dante, The. 7d.
Doré Gallery, The. 7d.
Edinburgh, Old and New. 7d.
Egypt: Descriptive, Historical, and Picturesque. 1s.
Encyclopædic Dictionary. 1s.
English Literature, Library of. 6d.
Family Physician, The. 6d.
Gardening, Cassell's Popular. 7d.
Garden Flowers, Familiar. 6d.
Geikie's Life and Words of Christ. 7d.
Gleanings from Popular Authors. 7d.
Great Industries of Great Britain. 7d.
Health, The Book of. 6d.
Horse, The Book of the. 1s.
Household Guide, Cassell's. 6d.
India, Cassell's History of. 7d.
Little Folks. 6d.
Greater London. 7d.
Longfellow's Poems. 7d.
Mechanics, Dictionary of. 7d.
Miniature Library of the Poets.* 1s.
Music, History of. 7d.
Natural History, Cassell's. 7d.
Old Testament Commentary.* Bishop Ellicott's. 7d.
Our Own Country. 7d.
Peoples of the World. 7d.
Picturesque Canada. 2s. 6d.
Picturesque Europe. 1s.
Pigeons, Illustrated Book of. 6d.
Popular Educator, Cassell's. 6d.
Protestantism, History of. 7d.
Quiver, The. 6d.
Red Library, Cassell's.* 1s. & 2s.
Russo-Turkish War, History of the. 7d.
Saturday Journal, Cassell's.* 6d. (Also Weekly, 1d.)
Science for All. 7d.
Life of Christ,* Farrar's. 6d.
Shakespeare, Cassell's. 7d.
Technical Educator, Cassell's. 6d.
Trees, Familiar. 6d.
Wild Birds, Familiar. 6d.
Wild Flowers, Familiar. 6d.

Cassell's Railway Time Tables and Through-Route Glance Guide. 4d.

All are Illustrated, except those indicated by an asterisk.

⁎⁎⁎ Particulars of the above will be found in Cassell & Company's *Complete Catalogue*, a copy of which will be forwarded post free on application to Cassell & Company, Limited, Ludgate Hill, London.

www.ingramcontent.com/pod-product-compliance
Lightning Source LLC
Chambersburg PA
CBHW020237170426
43202CB00008B/116